THE
LIVING
GODDESS

THE
LIVING
GODDESS

Reclaiming the Tradition
of the Mother of the Universe

Linda Johnsen

Yes International Publishers
Saint Paul, Minnesota

Portions of this book have appeared, in different forms, in *Yoga International, Yoga Journal* and *Light of Consciousness* magazines.

Quotation from Amritanandamayi Ma in Chapter 4: © 1997 by Mata Amritanandamayi Center. Used by permission. Excerpted from *AMRITANANDAM* - First Quarter 1997.

The lengthy quote from Swami Rama Bharati in Chapter 4 is adopted from *Sadhana: The Essence of Spiritual Life* by Swami Rama, Himalayan International Institute, New Delhi, India, 1996.

Translations from the *Tripura Rahasya* were completed with the invaluable assistance of Pandit Rajmani Tigunait.

Cover art is from an original painting by Eric Estep. Color prints of the painting are available from the artist 1787 Montecito, Mountain View, CA 94043, (650-960-1409).

All rights reserved.
Copyright © 1999 by Linda Johnsen
No part of this book may be reproduced or transmitted
in any form or by any means, electronic or mechanical,
including photocopying, recording, or
by any information storage and retrieval system,
without written permission from the publisher
except in the case of brief quotations
embodied in critical articles and reviews.
For information and permissions address:

Yes International Publishers
1317 Summit Avenue, Saint Paul, MN 55105-2602
651-645-6808

Library of Congress Cataloging-in-Publication Data

Johnsen, Linda, 1954 -
       The living goddess / Linda Johnsen
              p.   cm.
       Includes bibliographical references.
       ISBN 0-936663-23-5
       1. Goddesses —Hinduism.
  BL1216.2.J64   1999
  294.5' 2114—dc21   98-54147
                                            CIP

Printed in the United States of America

Acknowledgments

As we Norwegian-Americans say, *"Tusen takk!"* (a thousand thank you's) to Theresa King of Yes International Publishers for singlehandedly materializing this book. She is the best publisher any writer could dream of.

"Tusen takk" also to my many friends in the American yoga community who kept insisting that I sit down and finish this book. Whenever I found myself distracted by other projects, I could always count on impatient friends calling to demand, "Isn't your Goddess book done *yet?*"

And as my Indian friends say, *"Koti pranam!"* (I bow again and again) to Swami Rama Bharati, who came down from the Himalayas to try to enlighten skeptical, overly intellectual Westerners like me. He had his work cut out for him, yet no one could have been more perfectly suited for the job.

I bow again and again to Amritanandamayi Ma (Ammachi), who absolutely perfectly embodies the World Mother. To sit in her presence is to personally experience the living Goddess.

I bow again and again to Shree Maa of Kamakhya, who makes living in perfection and selfless love from moment to moment look natural and effortless.

And let me especially thank my husband Johnathan Brown, one of the few people I know who can stare directly into Mother Kali's eyes and keep his composure!

To the people of India
who have kept faith with the Goddess
— forever —

Table of Contents

1

Invoking the Goddess:
Entering the Universe of Tantra

APPROACHING THE GODDESS

The music is deafening. Brahmin priests are thundering on their drums as the screen separating us from the Goddess is pulled aside. She stands before us: the Mother of the Universe. Her skin is pitch black, her tongue lolls out of her mouth, her blood stained sword is poised to strike. Energy radiates from her fierce dark form like heat from a blast furnace. Kali Ma!

The local villagers, who have come to temples like this one to worship the Divine Mother every evening for thousands of years, are chanting her name, "Narayani, Narayani!" We are in Bengal now, the Goddess's ancient stomping grounds. She gazes intensely at her children, gathered here in the twilight.

The statue before us, into which a breath from the life force of the Cosmic Mother has been infused (living images like this one are pejoratively called "idols" by uncomprehending foreign missionaries), illuminates the tiny rural temple with blessings. Now the priests begin to chant. I recognize the Sanskrit words, borrowed from India's great tantric hymn, *Devi Mahatmyam* (The Glory of the Goddess).

> With loving devotion we bow to the Great Goddess,
> the eternal, auspicious, primordial cause
> and sustaining power of the universe!
> We bow again and again to the Mother of the World!

The form of the Goddess is horrible. Garlanded with human skulls, she is dancing on a corpse. But the energy emanating from her is loving, benign. Although several of her hands contain weapons, others are extended in traditional gestures of blessing. The Goddess contains everything in herself: good and evil, creation and destruction. Facing reality, acknowledging the savage grimness of life, can be a terrifying experience. Yet to those with the courage to look her in the eye, Kali signals with one of her four hands, "Fear not!" and with another, "I will protect you!"

The Divine Mother is often portrayed as a warrioress in the Hindu tradition. This iconography often baffles Westerners, who think of the Goddess—when they think of her at all—as sultry and venusian like Aphrodite, or as meekly long-suffering like the Virgin Mary. However, in India the Goddess is not a warrior in the male sense, glorying in conquest and plunder. I remember watching a male bear saunter up to a cub. This can be a horrifying scenario—male bears are known to kill cubs they didn't father. The mother, a dozen yards away, noticed the male approaching and in less than a second, literally faster than you can blink your eyes, she shot through the air in a raging attack. The male bear, twice her size, leapt in terror, swung around, and dashed into the forest as quickly as his legs could carry him. This is the kind of warrioress the Divine Mother is, and this is the kind of protection her Indian devotees expect.

To the villagers here tonight, sitting on the concrete floor in Kali's temple, the Goddess is their protectress. She is also nature itself, she is power, she is the mystery of birth and the terror of death, and still she is something more. It is the unlimited majesty of reality itself the children of Kali are here to worship.

The singing concludes, and devotees shuffle forward to touch the upraised foot of the Goddess. "Whatever you ask of Kali sincerely, with love in your heart, she will give you. Remember, she is your mother," a priest whispers as I approach.

It is awesome to come near the Goddess. While the energy pouring out of her feels benefic, it is nevertheless so powerful that like the warm, gentle waves of a calm sea, I could drown in it. Sanctity envelops her like incense. This particular image of Kali represents the Goddess who removes all obstacles which separate us from her. Humbly and a little nervously I place my right hand on her foot asking, "Mother, please take from me all shackles that bind me to a limited understanding of you, or of myself. Bind me with love for you." I glance up at her face, hoping she has heard me, and then hoping if she has that I was truly sincere. A smiling brahmin fills my palms with flower petals as I step away, back into the unfailing sunlight of Northern California.

I jolt awake, my heart wrenching with yearning. It's been years since I worshiped at the tiny temple outside Calcutta. I miss the innocent faith of the Hindu villagers, the ageless chants of the brahmin priests. Most of the churches I've visited here at home feel like barren wombs in comparison. How different the stiff Protestant hymns and self righteous sermonizing feel from the temples in India, where my breath stopped the moment I stepped in the door because pure, vibrant divinity was throbbing there. I remember a temple devoted to Raja Rajeshvari (The Supreme Sovereign Empress of the Universe) where ecstatic energy enveloped the statue of the Goddess palpably as a force field. There was also a Vaishnava temple where a small statue of the Earth Goddess Bhumeshvari stood blazing with power so physically tangible it made my body tingle. A fellow American turned to me wide-eyed; he felt it too.

I remember sitting with a pandit from Benares who described his beloved Goddess with so much devotion that she entered the room and sat down with us. I distinctly felt her presence; she was sitting behind me—if I had turned my head I might have seen her. And I remember moments in meditation that were sublime, moments when the entire universe seemed suffused with the Mother's smile.

I used to envy the Catholics when I was a child, because in their religion God had a mother. "When you're really in trouble," one of my girlfriends from Our Lady of Mercy confided, "pray to Mary. She always helps out." I used to wish Mary would appear to me like she did to the girl at Lourdes, but she never did—perhaps, I figured, because I was Lutheran.

It's easy for anyone—even stiff-lipped Norwegian Lutherans—to worship the Divine Mother in India. They know the Goddess intimately there. It's the one culture on earth which has been calling to her without ceasing from before the beginning of history. They know every facet of her personality and honor all of them, even the horrible ones.

Maha Devi, "the Great Goddess," appears in a myriad of forms throughout India. At Kanya Kumari (the southernmost extreme of the subcontinent) she is worshiped as Bala, a young girl. The capricious way in which she plays with our lives—ending one life prematurely here, granting someone else a sudden fortune there, sending abundant harvests, sending plague—reminds villagers of the way a willful child plays with her dolls. Call to her once and she comes running to your arms; call to her another time—call and call and call—and she doesn't come. Like a child, she's whimsical and utterly unpredictable, but it's impossible not to love her.

Maha Devi is Uma, the moon-faced yogini of the Himalayas, she is the white-skinned Gauri of the brahmins and the dark-skinned Kalika of the tantrics. She is Sheetala, Goddess of fever, in the tiny village temples of those who fear disease, Shantosi on the home altars of those who crave harmony and prosperity. She is Bhagavati (Blessed Goddess) in Kerala and Chamundeshvari (Conqueror of Evil) in Mysore. She's called Sarada in Sringeri and Kamakshi at Kanchipuram. At her shrine in Vindhyachal, near Benares, for century after century she's been worshiped as the bird-headed Goddess Vindhya Vasini. She is Chandika in Calcutta, Amba in Kashmir, and Bhavani in Maharashtra. In Madurai they call her Shyamala, in Brindaban she's Radha, and at Jambukeshvaram her name is Akhilandeshvari. In fact, the Divine Mother has so many names in India that it's a common practice for devotees to chant a *sahasranaman,* a set of a thousand of her names, as part of their morning worship—and there are many different sets of names to choose from.

And yet there's only one Goddess! Hindu scriptures explain that wherever you address your prayers, whether you send them to Kali, Kwan Yin, Tara or the Virgin Mary, they all get forwarded to the same mailbox. In a medieval Hindu classic called "The Mystery of the Triune Goddess," the Divine Mother explains, "Who and what I really am—cosmic awareness so vast I effortlessly hold trillions of universes in the palm of my hand—is beyond the capacity of human minds to understand. Therefore imagine me in whatever form appeals to you, and I promise in that very form I will come to you."

This is the reason you can travel the entire Indian subcontinent without meeting a single Hindu who's interested in converting you. They believe that whether you call the Supreme Being "Jehovah" or "Allah," "Krishna" or "Kali," the one who created you is holding you lovingly in her embrace and joyously accepts your worship. She assumes an infinite number of forms, including the many goddesses of the Hindu pantheon, in order to guide, guard, and enlighten us all, whatever our culture or religious tradition.

SHAKTISM: THE HEART OF TANTRA

The Hindu Goddess tradition is called Shaktism; the Goddess's devotees are called Shaktas. Shakti means the primordial, universal consciousness/energy which birthed the cosmos out of its limitless being and lovingly attends to the needs of each of its creatures. Therefore it is conceived as a feminine force. While many Westerners believe that God is literally male, as if he conceals an enormous sex organ under his toga, Shaktas say that when we call the matrix of being a Goddess, we have only begun to describe its infinite divine qualities, not that we have made some kind of final defining statement. Just as we human women have feminine characteristics but are much more than our gender, the Mother of the Universe is more than female. Her living being extends beyond the furthest reach of human imagination, beyond any limiting conception we project on her.

Christianity, Islam, Judaism, and (surprisingly) Buddhism, associate action with masculinity and passivity with femininity. In Shaktism, God (Shiva) is the silent, unmoving one over whose prostrate body the Goddess rampages; she (Shakti) is dynamic, self-willed energy. And then again, the Goddess is the primordial unchanging universal awareness which enjoys the swirling movements of her beloved, Shiva Nataraja, whose dance of creation and destruction begins and ends world systems. God and Goddess interchange passive and active roles like lovers, unrestricted by human definitions.

Years ago when I asked a Shakta whether she believed in God or a Goddess, she swiveled her head in that common, exasperating Indian gesture which means both yes and no. "There is one mother from whom all of us come out. In my tradition we call that one Maha Tripura Sundari, which means the beautiful Goddess who lives outside the three states of matter, mind and spirit, but who also lives inside them. She experiences all events to be happening all at once, and experiences all of us to be part and parcel of herself. You and I, though, feel we are two separate beings rather than one integrated consciousness. From our point of view we say there is God Shiva, the divine consciousness, and Goddess Shakti. Shiva is always immersed in meditation, but Shakti likes to play, so she created all these worlds. She created the game of suffering and enjoyment, ignorance and enlightenment. She is the source of all blessings, material and spiritual, so in our tradition we approach the Goddess for her grace, much like young children approach their mother. So yes there is a God and a Goddess, but only so long as we retain the point of view of duality. In deep states of meditation the sages experience that God and Goddess are not two separate entities, but one divine being, the Supreme Goddess Maha Tripura Sundari."

Shaktas believe in karma and reincarnation. They tell the story that at one time God (Shiva) and Goddess (Shakti) were happily married, living together at the top of Mount Kailash in Tibet. But then Daksha, a haughty sage, insulted Shiva, saying he was lazy—sitting in meditation all the time instead of getting a good job, and poor—because he wants and owns nothing. The Goddess was so angry at Daksha, she built a fire and immolated herself in protest. God Shiva clung to his wife's corpse in a frenzy of grief, but everywhere he stepped another piece of her body fell away. After many eons, the Goddess incarnated as Parvati, daughter of the mountains, and did intense spiritual practices to win Shiva back as her husband.

At one time, the story is saying, you and I dwelt in perfect union with Shiva—divine being. Then the "insulting" thought arose that a life in union with God was not enough; that in order to be fulfilled we must experience material life as well, work and wealth, owner-ship and responsibility, passion and pain. You and I, who were one being then, not two, immolated ourself in matter. We lost our unity then, disintegrating into separate entities who no longer experience the cosmos as one vast, intelligent, interconnected whole. That is why we never seem to be completely fulfilled; we are haunted by the sense that we are more than what we presently experience ourselves to be. So we begin to practice the intense disciplines of spiritual life called *tapas*—burning—in India, in order to reunite ourselves with our one true love, God himself. We incarnate over and over again, in human and non-human forms, as we burn our way back to full consciousness of our union with God. The entire universe is the Goddess's cremation ground, the tantrics say.

DARWIN MEETS THE MOTHER OF THE UNIVERSE

The Shakta worldview is radically different from that of Western science. In the mid-1970s I was astonished to hear Swami Rama Bharati, a well known Shakta master from North India, attack Darwin's theory of evolution. "We have been watching apes for thousands of years. Who has ever seen an ape turn into a man? Never believe it!" Swamiji was not an uneducated fundamentalist. He was an advanced yogi who, under laboratory conditions, demonstrated extraordinary conscious control over his heart beat, body temperature and brain waves. He respected the methodology of modern science—its emphasis on basing one's beliefs on a foundation of replicable experiments and practical experience was similar to the approach behind the *vidyas* or sacred sciences of the yogis and yoginis in his own Himalayan community—but he completely rejected the notion that evolution is driven by chance or blind necessity.

We in the West are told the cosmos is material and consciousness is its epiphenomenon. The Swami, like all Shaktas, believes the cosmos is consciousness, and that matter is its epiphenomenon. There is a living, intelligent organizing principle which drives evolution in this world as well as in all the subtle interpenetrating worlds that coexist with ours. Shakta scriptures, based on traditions thousands of years old, agree with Western science that the Earth is billions of years old, but when human beings or any other species come into existence, it is because the divine force wills it, not because an ape randomly mutates into human form. Nature is the play of Shakti, the Goddess, who is living, self-aware, and limitlessly powerful.

Interestingly, in recent years Darwin's mechanistic interpretation of evolution has increasingly come under fire. In the century and a half since Darwin formulated his theory that new species develop from old ones through "survival of the fittest," scientists have examined millions of fossils; not one example of the transitional life forms postulated by Darwin has ever been confirmed. Darwinists today believe that evolution also occurs through the accidental mutation of genetic structure. Yet humans have been breeding animals and plants since at least 6000 B.C.; in that time not one example of a species "mutating" into another has ever been reported. Even in laboratories where researchers use rapidly reproducing insects and microorganisms, manipulating their environment and even irradiating them in an effort to force the genetic mutations allegedly required to produce a new species, the specimens eventually become deformed or sterile and die out; *never* has a new species been seen to emerge.

Darwin assumed that once a prototypical organ such as a primitive eye had evolved, it would be comparatively easy for more sophisticated eyes to develop. Today, scientists ruefully admit that the biochemistry involved in such a transition would be so phenomenally complex, it's physically impossible for it to occur in a random manner without the eye ceasing to be an eye! As for the famous examples of evolution in action Darwin believed he observed in the Galapagos Islands, recent research has revealed that Darwin's famous finches are one interbreeding species, not separate species evolved from a common ancestor as he mistakenly supposed. The last decade has seen frantic biologists scrambling to develop new versions of evolutionary theory in an effort to shore up the tottering edifice of Darwinism. One prominent Harvard based paleontologist has offered a theory called "punctuated equilibrium," according to which evolution simply stops for hundreds of millions of years, then mystically, magically starts up again for a brief spurt before mysteriously halting once more. This, he feels, explains the lack of evidence for Darwinian-style evolution in the fossil record and the laboratory. His theory is perhaps the clearest measure of how desperate Darwinists are becoming.

Scientists explain that conditions on Earth could not support organic life till about 3.8 billion years ago. After that point it would have required hundreds of millions of years for even the simplest protein molecule to form randomly, and perhaps another billion more before a single one-celled organism might randomly develop. Yet in 1979 geologists discovered fossils of yeast-like organisms in Greenland dating back 3.8 billion years! Apparently from the first moment life was possible, it instantly appeared. These and numerous other embarrassing anomalies in the fossil record have left scientists wide open to attack from Creationists, who insist that the story of creation detailed in the Bible is literally true.

After claiming Darwin was wrong, Swami Rama Bharati explained the Shakta version of evolution, a view halfway between Western science and fundamentalist Christianity. Shaktism, like the yoga tradition in general, has always taught that the Earth is billions of years old and that something like evolution does in fact occur, not only in the physical world but also spiritually. Shaktism does not accept, however, that the character of living beings is determined by their genes alone. Behind the physical body lies the *pranamaya kosha*, "the body made of life-force," which shapes the development of the physical body from the moment of conception. The phantom limb phenomenon in which individuals whose limbs have been amputated continue to vividly feel the missing arm or leg, suggests that although the physical part is missing, the organizing force behind it continues to exist. This organizing field cannot be perceived by the eyes but continues to be sensed by the brain. Ancient Indian scientists called this life energy *prana*, ancient Chinese scientists called it *chi*, ancient Egyptian scientists called it *ka*, and medieval European scientists called it the vital force. Of the advanced civilizations which have arisen throughout history, the modern West alone has not yet discovered this force.

A still more subtle type of energy pervades the body of prana. This is the *manomaya kosha*, "the body made of mind." Because one's thoughts and feelings interpenetrate one's vital force and physical body, your feelings can help make your body sick or well, while the health of your body affects your mental condition. Still more subtle bodies underlie the mind. These are the *vijnanamaya kosha*, "the body made of intuitive power," and the *anandamaya kosha,* "the body made of bliss," which is experienced in ecstatic mystical states. These last two bodies are the vehicles of the reincarnating soul and carry the individual's baggage of karma from life to life. It is one's karma which determines one's character and talents in this life, according to the Shaktas, not one's genes.

Shaktas say all the worlds, and all the souls in all the worlds, were consciously projected out of herself by the Divine Mother. The Goddess is not a mythological figurine in this system; she is the living matrix from which the universe springs. Our cosmos evolves not at the prompting of random chance, but in accordance with the shaktis, the intelligent energies, continually emanating from the divine matrix. This womb of being is a limitless source of energy, so Shaktas believe that our cosmos is filled with a infinite number not just of galaxies but of entire universes, though as long as we limit our level of consciousness to what we can perceive through our senses, we are aware of only one universe, our own. The great Shakta masters are men and women who live in full awareness of the Goddess's living presence on all planes of reality.

The Mother of the Universe is more than a genetrix to Shaktas, however. She is always brimming over with *ananda lahari,* "waves of bliss," something very much like what we humans call love. With great delight she sends her children out into the worlds to play, and when it's time for them to come home, she lovingly gathers them back into her arms. She is also called guru shakti, for she guides each soul on its journey through the worlds, teaching it the inner truths of its nature, testing its mettle, and training it to become a *jivanmukta,* a being of love and knowledge who moves through the realms of creation in freedom and fearlessness. This journey is not mythologic to Shaktas, for their history is filled with true stories of men and women who the Goddess actually transformed into *paramahansas,* "perfect swans." To this day India remains a spawning ground for saints and genuine spiritual masters. It is for the evolution of consciousness that the Mother emanated the world.

There's a very famous story in the *Mahabharata,* one of India's ancient epics, about Draupadi, a North Indian queen honored to this day as a human incarnation of the Great Goddess. King Duryodhana wanted to rape her, but as his thugs tore off her sari, more fabric kept appearing around her body. Finally the attackers gave up in exhaustion, as heaps of cloth laid piled around them on the floor, and yet still the queen remained completely clothed. That night Draupadi went in to her husband Yudhishthira, slipped out of her sari, and gave herself to him completely. It seems scientists—those who seek to unveil the secrets of nature so they can exploit her—uncover one layer of reality only to discover another, as the Ptolemic paradigm gave way to the Newtonian, the Newtonian to the Einsteinian, that to the quantum mechanical, and on and on. Mystics, however, do not rely on their limited rational minds to penetrate the Goddess's inner sanctum. Instead they make love to her with their whole souls, worshipping her with tears of adoration. The Shaktas say that only before her sincerest lovers does the Goddess unveil herself: it is the yogis and devotees to whom she reveals her mysteries.

THE LIVING TRADITION

Shaktism can be traced to neopaleolithic times; archeologists have unearthed Goddess figurines in the earliest strata of Indian settlements. Shaktism had enormous impact throughout much of Asia, profoundly affecting every sect of Hinduism as well as other religions rooted in Indian soil such as Buddhism and Jainism. Shakta-like concepts and practices also permeate Chinese Taoism. Major Shakta texts surviving to the present day include the voluminous *Devi Bhagavatam Purana* (Ancient Annals of the Luminous Goddess), *Tripura Rahasya* (The Mystery of the Triune Goddess), *Lalita Mahatmyam* (The Greatness of the Goddess) and *Saundarya Lahari Ananda Lahari* (Waves of Beauty, Waves of Bliss). There are thousands of other authoritative scriptures in the tradition, a veritable treasure trove of mystical literature devoted to the Goddess.

Today just as 10,000 years ago, images of the Goddess are everywhere in India. You'll find them painted on the sides of trucks, pasted to the dashboard of taxis, postered on the walls of shops. You'll often see a color painting of the Goddess prominently displayed in Hindu homes. Usually the picture is hung high on the wall so you have to crane your neck backwards, looking up toward her feet.

What a different situation from the West! It's difficult to

imagine now, but twenty years ago hardly anyone in America was aware the Goddess tradition even existed, much less that it pervaded much of the ancient world. In 1983 I first consulted *Books in Print,* the bible of the publishing industry, hoping to track down material about female deities. There was so little information available in English that, although page after page of titles were listed under the heading "God," *Books in Print* didn't bother to include an entry for "Goddess"!

Thanks to the work of brilliant feminist researchers like Merlin Stone and Marija Gimbutas, this situation has improved dramatically. Today books with the word "Goddess" in the title outsell books about "God" in many shops. And yet most Westerners, even many interested in women's spirituality, are unaware that an authentic, unbroken Goddess religion is still practiced by millions of devotees in South Asia. What little they know of this ancient venerable tradition is culled from films like *Indiana Jones and the Temple of Doom* where devotees of the Goddess are portrayed as psychotic cultists who rip hearts out of living victims. A recent popular novel titled *The Song of Kali* by an award-winning science fiction writer depicts Calcutta—a city in which I lived—as the cesspool of humanity and Bengali followers of the Goddess as power-crazy serial killers who slice open human babies. This is the way our arts and media present the most beautiful, profound and sacred Goddess religion on Earth! It may behoove us to remember that the largest film industry in the world is not in Hollywood—it's in Bombay. I wonder how we Westerners would react if Hindus started making movies depicting Christians and Jews the way we depict worshipers of the Goddess in India!

What is Goddess religion really like in South Asia? Forget the lurid books and movies. Picture instead a Goddess tradition that had flourished for thousands of years before our own Western civilization was even born, and that continued to thrive uninterruptedly while the Goddess religions of our own culture were systematically annihilated. The depth and magnitude of the Shakta tradition is immense—almost, to the Western mind, inconceivable. It has been practiced and elaborated by millions of sincere seekers since time immemorial, by the humblest of the poor as well as by some of the most brilliant minds who ever graced this planet. It has inspired saints, yogis and yoginis, artists, and the pure hearts of the simplest villagers of the Indian culture almost forever. Many of the most influential Indian saints of modern times were Shaktas, including Ramakrishna Paramahansa, Swami Vivekananda, Paramahansa Yogananda, Sri Aurobindo and Amritanandamayi Ma. For ten days twice each year all of Hindu India becomes Shakta during Nava Ratri, a festival celebrating the supremacy of the three immensely popular goddesses Sarasvati, Lakshmi and Durga.

Many deities are worshipped in India, including the male gods Shiva (the supreme yogi who is always immersed in meditation and therefore is sometimes equated with consciousness itself), Vishnu (who incarnated on earth as the heroes Rama and Krishna), Ganesha (the one with an elephant's head—elephants being considered not only the mightiest but the most intelligent and compassionate of creatures by the Indian people), and Skanda (a warrior against evil who is, like Ganesha, a son of Shiva and the beloved Goddess Parvati). Yet the Goddess remains enormously popular. All Hindu devotees of male gods acknowledge the Goddess. The construction of a temple to a male deity without the inclusion at least one image of the Goddess is literally unthinkable to the Hindu mind.

I remember driving through Kerala, India's southwestern-most province, where Christianity has gained a foothold. I didn't see a single statue of Jesus. Yet consecrated statues of Mary, the blue-robed Mother of God, were everywhere. Even among the converted, the Great Goddess continues to hold sway.

For a Westerner like me, raised from my first breath in a milieu in which every emblem of the divine without exception is emphatically male, travelling through India—surrounded at every step by Goddess imagery and continually hearing the name of the Divine Mother chanted in homes and on the streets—was a remarkable and deeply moving experience. In India Goddess worship is not a "cult," it's a religion. There millions of people turn every day with heartfelt yearning to the Mother of the Universe. Even here in the comparatively enlightened burg of California, when we sponsor a Goddess celebration, participants are almost exclusively female; men seem somehow to think that Goddess worship is a phenomenon unique to "women's spirituality." In India

50% of the participants at any Goddess festival are male, as well they should be. Hindu men have simply never learned that the Goddess isn't relevant to them. Thankfully, the most ancient religion in the world still finds a home in the Hindu heart.

RETURN TO THE GODDESS

The last twenty years have seen a powerful resurgence of interest in the Goddess here in the West. We're reading about Greek and Roman goddesses—even Sumerian goddesses—yet there's been surprisingly little interest in the goddesses of India. Since childhood we've been taught to respect the Greeks and Romans as the forebears of our civilization, and to look down on the starving nameless masses of India. Fortunately for them, we have heroines like Mother Teresa we can send to save them from their ignorance and squalor! What could these superstitious, dark skinned people possibly have to teach us?

We think of India as a third world basket case, forgetting that 500 years ago some of the most backward and illiterate countries on the planet were the primitive monarchies of Europe, where kings and queens eagerly commissioned explorers like Columbus to search for a sea route to the most wealthy and cultured civilization of its day: India. India had been the goal of merchants since at least Sumerian times, more than 4,000 years ago. Many Westerners still consider Sumeria and Egypt to be the cradles of human civilization, yet recent excavations have revealed a flourishing ancient culture in greater North India which extended 1600 kilometers from east to west, and 1400 kilometers from north to south. Think about that for a minute. If you dropped the entire ancient Egyptian and Mesopotamian civilizations into that land area, they would barely fill a corner. Some of the cities in India circa 2600 B.C. were more sophisticated than any city anywhere in Europe till 1700 A.D.

Remember also that Roman civilization had such an enormous trade deficit to India that Roman emperors through the time of Hadrian were continually at war with the Parthians, trying to punch a hole through Persia in the hope of delivering more of their own wares to the far wealthier Indians. The Arabs (who kept intellectual inquiry alive in the West while Christian Europe plunged into the

Dark Ages) considered India the birthplace of philosophy, astronomy and mathematics.

More recently, a series of foreign invasions, and wholesale unabashed looting by the British Raj, eventually reduced India to poverty. The Europeans helped themselves to the vast wealth of the subcontinent, but not to its wisdom. Since freeing itself of British rule in 1947, the Indians have pulled their country up by its bootstraps, restoring prosperity to much of the subcontinent. Unfortunately the legacy of the earlier Islamic invasion continues to haunt India, as Muslims and Hindus struggle to come to terms. Muslim fundamentalists destroyed innumerable Goddess temples in their efforts to annihilate India's ancient faith. Then the British demanded Hindus accept Christianity in order to qualify for better jobs.

But the Europeans did more than sack India: they actually fabricated a new history for it. Light-skinned European "Aryans" supposedly invaded India some 3,500 years ago, driving the help-less native Dravidian people across the Vindhya mountains into South India, as well as imposing patriarchy in their bloody Aryan wake. Unfortunately feminist authors have helped perpetuate this historical hallucination, having made the catastrophic error of basing their conclusions regarding the spread of patriarchy on the racist work of 19th and 20th century male European Orientalists.

Today we know that the Dravidian people have always been exactly where they themselves insist they've always lived: in South India. Their ancestors came not from the north, as Western historians used to claim, but from the south, as their own legends report. Indo-European peoples did not enter North India in 1500 B.C., but have lived there, as their own historical records document, for at the very least the last 6,000 years. Goddess worship didn't seep into Indian civilization from tribal areas around the 9th century A.D., as Western scholars used to imagine, but has been an integral part of Indian culture since prehistoric times, as many an archeological site testifies, and as the Shaktas themselves have always stated. European efforts to "rewrite" Indian history are a spectacular example of the Western attempt to erase the Goddess from history!

Unfortunately, in many parts of the world, the Mother of the Universe did vanish. While the Greeks and the Romans lost their goddesses, however, India hung on. Yet we in the West have been slow to turn to the wisdom of India for insights into the Goddess. Why?

"Eastern religions are too focused on the transcendent. We've had 2,000 years of that. We need to come back down to the earth, to our bodies, to our desires. We have to stop listening to gurus who tell us this world is an illusion, that we should all go to the mountains and meditate. I want to be happy right here, right now!"

I'm always flabbergasted by the claim that Westerners need to free themselves from a transcendent conception of God. From the Shakta point of view, the West has not been steeped in transcendentalism for the past 2,000 years, rather it's completely forgotten what the transcendent is! Living divinity has become an old man sitting in the sky tabulating our sins. He is there, we are here; he is holy, we are sinful. The perspective of the Shaktas is radically different. Living divinity is completely transcendent, but it is also a mother. It projected us out of the womb of its own being. It is not as if God is separate from us, or even that God is somehow distantly connected to us; from the Shakta point of view every particle in our body, every sensation in our mind, our innermost soul, everything all around us, is completely sacred, partaking fully of the transcendent divine.

According to Shaktism the world itself is not an illusion but *maya* in the most ancient sense of the term: the Goddess's glory. However, it is our understanding of the world which is often riddled with illusions. Any time we look outside ourselves or inside ourselves and see anything less than the all pervading Goddess, any time we experience anything other than her perfect bliss, we are misperceiving the true nature of things, Shaktas believe. This is *avidya,* our ignorance, and it is only our ignorance that separates us from the Goddess. While each yogic lineage in India uses slightly different terminology to describe it, this basic understanding is at the root of all tantric practice.

Tantra—now there's a loaded word. In the West many people seriously believe that Tantra means celebrating sexuality. In America yoga, the Sanskrit word for union with God, means standing on one's head, and Tantra means holding one's breath while assuming complicated sexual postures. Americans have a remarkable capacity for oversimplifying and commercializing the sacred truths of other traditions. Perhaps this is why many Native Americans (called Indians to this day because Columbia believed he'd reached his destination—India) refuse to share their religious practices with well intentioned but patronizing neo-American would-be students.

THE TANTRIC UNIVERSE

Since Tantra is so closely associated with the Goddess tradition, it is important to clarify what it actually means. Tantra is a meditative tradition designed to evoke in the practitioner the living reality of the divinity of all things. Its exalted worldview and demanding psychological techniques are exhaustively described in 10th century classics such as the *Tantra Loka* (The Light of Tantra) and the *Tantra Sara* (The Ocean of Tantra). As part of one's spiritual practice, he or she maintains a meditative focus in order to make sacred even the ordinary acts of life, such as eating, working, making love, or breathing.

It's unfortunate that so often writers popularizing Tantra in the West perpetuate the myth that Tantra means yogic sex. As anyone who's actually been to India knows, one has to sift through literally hundreds of tantric texts before finding even one that deals with sexuality. Those who take sensationalized books on Eastern mysticism seriously and seek out a tantric guru in India, expecting detailed instructions in sexual techniques, are in for quite a shock— few tantrics deal with this subject at any length and, for better or worse, quite a few of them advise celibacy! Fortunately, in the context of lay people's lives, the yoga tradition broadens the definition of celibacy *(brahmacharya)* to limiting one's sexual activities to one partner with whom he or she is engaged in a loving and committed relationship. In this manner one's sexual energy is simultaneously expressed, disciplined, and directed toward the divine.

Spiritualized sex is an important but comparatively minor part of the tantric tradition as a whole. These days, however, there is actually a cottage industry in India composed of artists who produce erotic paintings and prints to cater to Western tourists, who pay absurd sums for what they naively believe are authentic medieval Indian representations of advanced tantric practices.

The correct Sanskrit term for that which many Westerners erroneously believe to be Tantra is *kama,* as in the famous Indian manual on sexuality and self-culture called the *Kama Sutra. Kama* is the force of desire, whether it be the desire that drives people toward sexual union, or the desire that motivates the Supreme Being to manifest the universe. One of the names of the Goddess is Kameshvari, the "Supreme Empress of Desire," for it is from her this force in all its forms originally springs. It's important to note, however, that Kameshvari is only one of her names: the Goddess has thousands of others, and very few of them have anything to do with sexuality.

Painfully often I've seen pandits and *sadhus,* authentic practitioners of the tantric tradition, wince when approached by enthusiastic but misinformed Western students asking to learn about "yogic sex." For the tantrics themselves, Tantra means uncovering the undying reality within oneself through meditation, yoga, ritual, selfless service, art, study, self-inquiry, and especially through devotion to the divine in whatever form one conceives of her. Authentic tantric teachers are looking for students who want to experience and serve the divine in all things. This is the motivation you need to have when you approach an advanced tantric teacher if you hope for a serious response.

I've often wondered why Westerners are so quick to associate Tantra, and particularly Shakta Tantra, with sexual practices. It may be because our Western notion of the Goddess has been primarily of a "fertility" icon, probably because Western archeologists reflexively associate the Divine Mother with the Earth, agriculture, the womb, childbirth. Western feminists and Goddess enthusiasts have championed this conception in their worthy efforts to resacrilize the "female" compartments of life such as sensuality and menses. However, anyone who wants to understand what the Mother Goddess means in India has to let go of this fertility-related conception. My personal suspicion is that we're not going to get to the root of our own lost Goddess tradition here in the West until we look into the deeper subtleties of what feminine divinity represents, as the tantrics have.

The existence since Vedic times, 6,000 years ago, of deities like

Sarasvati reveals that from the inception of Indian culture the Goddess was also associated with intelligence, creativity and refinements of civilization like philosophy, music and art. Deities like Kali and Durga illuminate the Goddess's close connection with both martial and spiritual might. And the esoteric lineages of Shaktism reveal mystical aspects of the Goddess many Western anthropologists hardly conceive of. The Goddess is not just about fertility. In Tantra she is primarily seen as the anthropomorphization of the spontaneous activity of universal consciousness, the force that called the universe into existence, which speaks to us through the inherent meaningfulness of events in our lives.

The tantrics I met in India were, almost without exception, devout spiritual aspirants performing their practices with incredible humility and self-discipline. For New Agers, however, Tantra seems to be about enhancing power, pleasure, and self-identity. For Shakta practitioners, on the contrary, it's about expanding beyond the ego. I respect the New Ager's characteristically Western pleasure-oriented approach to spirituality, but I'm deeply interested in learning the Shakta perspective. The Hindu Goddess tradition is millennia old and is in many ways an extraordinarily spiritually and psychologically mature tradition. Therefore when I use the word Tantra I am referring to the tradition as it's practiced in its original cultural context, not as the neo-Tantra advertised in New Age magazines.

GODDESS OF THE EAST / GODDESS OF THE WEST

Some Western Goddess enthusiasts sincerely feel it is more appropriate for us to study the Greek, Roman and even Egyptian goddesses, goddesses of "our" tradition, rather than multi-armed Hindu goddesses. In reality the distinction between Western and South Asian civilization is not so clear cut. After all, many Indians, like the majority of Americans, are Caucasians and speak Indo-European languages. Ethnically, linguistically and historically India is not so much a distant neighbor as an elder sister.

In the West women are now trying to piece "our" Goddess tradition back together literally from a few shards of clay dug from ancient sites which bear testimony to a once great religion, and are recreating a Goddess mythology based on our modern needs and insights. Yet in India, from the most ancient times, the Goddess's esoteric tradition has remained intact. I can't help wondering whether if we were to look to India, we might not find a reflection of the inner dimension of Western Goddess religion which has been lost almost entirely, and which might add immeasurably to the depth and breadth of the Goddess faith now being created anew in Europe, Australia and the Americas.

Can we find glimmerings of the hidden spiritual content of the Western Goddess traditions in our sister tradition in India? I believe we can. In 1945 two peasants broke open a jar lying along the south face of a boulder near Nag Hammadi in Egypt. In it they found tattered manuscripts nearly 2,000 years old. They had stumbled upon what scholars would soon call the Nag Hammadi library, early Christian texts dating back to the time the biblical Gospels themselves were being composed. The texts reveal a radically different understanding of the Goddess's place in early Christianity than I was taught in Sunday school. Perhaps the most fascinating of these manuscripts is "Thunder, Perfect Mind," the poignant testament of Isis spoken just as humanity is turning away from the Goddess. The text is entirely tantric. The resonances with Indian goddesses are unmistakable. I don't think it a fluke that the Celts worshipped a Kali-like goddess of destruction called Cailleach or that their "Green Man" so closely resembles India's Shiva Pashupati. We may do well, therefore, to look to Shaktism for clues about what the original Western Goddess tradition may have been like. There exists the tantalizing possibility that Indian Shaktism represents not only an offshoot of the primeval Goddess faith, but its source.

Let me offer an explicit example. My Indo-European ancestors in Norway believed in a world tree called Yggdrasill. At the bottom of the tree lay the joyless netherworld called Hel (to which the English word "hell" is related). At the center of the tree lay our human world, Midgard, the "middle region." At the top part of the tree flourished Asgard, the "land of the gods." Near the top an eagle perched, its wings outspread. From its perch, dew showered down over the rest of the tree, refreshing and enlivening it. At the very bottom of the tree lay a coiled snake, always trying to strike the eagle far above it. At the very top sat Odin, the one-eyed king of the gods, surveying his domain.

Another ancient culture where the world tree is a dominant religious image is, of course, Hindu India. The central spiritual practice of Shaktism is kundalini yoga. The Shakta world tree represents the human spine. Toward the bottom of the spine lie the chakras associated with our animal urges: self-preservation, reproduction, and aggression, our "lower" nature, our personal "Hel." In the middle region of the spine lies the heart chakra, reflecting the capacity to love and relate selflessly to others—the human world or middle region. The chakras above the heart represent our divine capabilities: creativity, intellect/intuition, and mystical absorption, "the land of the gods." Behind and between our eyebrows lies the "third eye," represented by a circle from which two wings spread out, as if from an eagle. From this area *soma,* the elixir of consciousness, drips into the body, producing health and ecstacy. At the bottom of the spine lies the serpent kundalini, barely awake in most of us, whose purpose is to strike upwards, reaching the center between the eyebrows, elevating our lowest energies and connecting them with our highest aspirations. Shiva resides at the topmost chakra, representing our own Higher Self, watching, guiding, guarding, testing us. When Shakti, the kundalini, is reunited with Shiva, enlightenment occurs. Did old Norse shamans retain this understanding of the inner dimensions of Yggdrasill, the world tree? I suspect they did.

Our old Norse word for deity, *Aesir,* is the same as the ancient Indian term for God, *Asura.* In ancient times we Scandinavians, as well as the Germans and English, worshipped groups of goddesses called "the Mothers," just as in India to this day villagers worship the female *matris* (Sanskrit for "mothers"). Goddesses such as Nerthus (Mother Earth, Bhumeshvari in India), Nehalennia (Goddess of Good Fortune, Indian Sri), Freya (Goddess of Wealth and Sensuality, Indian Lakshmi), and the Norns ("the Fates") played pivotal roles in traditional Norse religion. When Christianity was forced on the Norwegian people by converted Vikings (who would go through households systemically killing each family member until the survivors agreed to be baptized), old gods like Odin and Thor were demonized, and the memory of the great Scandinavian goddesses was almost completely extinguished.

Lutheranism is Norway's state-supported religion. Not surprisingly, children in Norwegian schools today are taught that the coming of Christianity put an end to the brutal Viking era by wiping out the terrible old gods. In reality, the reign of the Vikings was a short aberration in Scandinavian history; for most of our history we Norwegians were comparatively peaceful people, despite our reverence for "violent" Indo-European gods and goddesses, just as the Jews have been a relatively peaceful people despite their belief in the "violent" God of the Torah. For most of our history the majority of Scandinavians didn't use Thor's hot-temperedness as an excuse for violent behavior, but understood his actions to represent the "violent" forces of nature such as thunder and lightning. It was Norway's rising merchant class which called for an end to banditry around 1000 A.D., ending the two centuries of murder and looting now affectionately remembered as the Viking period.

Was an esoteric tradition, which may have included Shakta practices such as working with kundalini, extinguished when the old religion of Europe was wiped out? Was the tradition of Europe's ancient goddesses originally charged with mystical insight, as the Indian Goddess tradition still is today? It's impossible to say for sure now, but the fact that the Yggdrasill imagery (to give just one example) is entirely Shakta, is extremely suggestive.

For most of human existence, Goddess worship could be found everywhere. While many scholars prefer to believe it was a fertility cult, I find it far more plausible that for many of its followers, this "Goddess cult" contained then, as now, an inner, deeply spiritual dimension. The oldest complete surviving scriptures we have today are India's *Vedas,* which are redolent with this inner understanding. The *Vedas* reveal that for at least as far back as we have records, devotees sought the transcendent aspect of the Goddess through prayer, meditation, asceticism, herbs, ritual, and many other types of yogic and shamanic methods. Today in the West we are reconnecting with the outermost visage of the Mother: her energies of fecundity, emotion, passion, physicality, and wish fulfillment. As our relationship with the Goddess matures perhaps we will also seek the dimension of her being which the Indians never lost—the all pervading, self-transcending consciousness/energy of the primordial Shakti.

I compiled this collection of the Divine Mother's teachings

about herself, culled from the Shakta tradition, for other Westerners like myself who want to know the Goddess better. I believe that the incredibly ancient and deeply mature Goddess spirituality of India can provide guidance for our own deepening appreciation of feminine divinity.

I also strongly feel we must turn to the living Goddess herself for deeper insight into her religion. Let the old lady speak for herself! One of the most respected Indian scholars of all time was the 10th century genius Abhinava Gupta who would often select a passage from a tantric text to explain in greater detail. One of his longest and most erudite commentaries was on two words: *Devi uvaccha* (the Goddess speaks). What does it mean to say the Goddess speaks? What language does she speak in? Sanskrit? *Sandhya Bhashan* (the twilight language)? Hebrew? Coptic? Does she use words at all? Sometimes the Shakta texts merely state, "The Goddess spoke like thunder in the sky of the mind." Maybe we need to look less to pot shards unearthed at archeological sites for clues about the Mother. Maybe we need to let her thunder a little in the receptive silence of our minds. There are thousands of scriptures in India written by devotees who listened, and are still listening, like the ancient devotees of Isis, to the thunder of perfect mind. In these texts the Goddess herself unmistakably, and awesomely, speaks. I'd like to share some of these tantric texts—her actual words—with you. May the living Goddess be heard!

Om Gam Ganeshaya Namah!
May all obstacles to the fulfillment of this resolution be removed!

Om Nava Grahebhyoh Namah!
May the planets be propitious to this endeavor!

Ya Devi Sarva Bhuteshu Matri Rupena Samsthita
Namastasyai Namastasyai Namastasyai Namo Namah!
I bow to the Supreme Goddess who abides in all beings
in the form of the Mother.
To that great Mother of all things,
I bow again and again!

2

SARASVATI
The Goddess as Wisdom and Inspiration

THE GODDESS IN THE ROAD

Traffic has come to a dead stop. I lean out over the door of our auto-rickshaw, trying to see what's holding us up. Normally, three-wheeled taxis like mine sprint between belching diesel trucks, the behemoths that edge out carts, cows, and hundreds of dark haired, dark skinned pedestrians, the 20th century A.D. elbowing the 20th century B.C. off the crowded, dusty Bihari street. It's hard to see through the mass of people and plumes of auto exhaust. We're trapped in gridlock so wildly chaotic, this could only be India.

Then in the distance I hear the shouting: *"Sarasvati ki jai!"* (Victory to the Goddess of Wisdom!) Of course! I lose track of time when I'm in India—a country where centuries can pass without anyone noticing—and I'd forgotten today is Sarasvati Puja, one of several annual holidays in which all Hindu India celebrates the Mother of the Universe. Back in California when we want to honor the Divine Mother, twenty or thirty of us get together in a New Age bookstore and hold a program. Here in India, 600,000,000 Hindus pour out into the streets shouting the Mother's names. Now this is what I call a Goddess festival! *"Sarasvati—"*

"Ki jai!" I join in the call. A young boy standing beside my taxi lifts his squirter and blasts me with red powder. It's all over my face, my hair, my dusty Punjabi travel outfit. We both laugh as he flings himself back into the celebration. Colored powder is flying everywhere; the air is giddy with jubilation.

Then the Goddess herself appears, clad in radiant white, playing her lute, while her extra hands clasp the book she's composed and the rosary on which she recites her own name. She is mature, beautiful, tranquil and luminous. Beside her feet, a white swan serenely surveys the crowd.

It was Sarasvati who projected our universe at the beginning of this cycle of creation, and whose unlimited creative energy erupts fresh every moment in the form of music and poetry, insight and ecstacy. The laws of physics are evidence of her boundless creative intelligence, though she herself is not fettered by these laws. The *Rig Veda,* India's 6,000 year-old bible, salutes Her as Vak, "the Word," because she manifests entire world systems merely by uttering a command. The primeval vibration of Sarasvati's will set the galaxies spinning.

Jubilant children are carrying the Mother of the Universe to the river in a palanquin strewn with flowers. Today is especially for them because on Sarasvati Puja, the Goddess—who contains all knowledge within the folds of her gown—is visiting earth with the special intention of blessing their studies. They have the day off from school to honor her, even as she manifests in the form of their own burgeoning intellects. Everyone is laughing and hollering as the Divine Mother approaches. My driver edges our auto-rickshaw to the side of the road so she can pass by.

This is what the teachers in the fundamentalist Christian school I attended as a child, disdainfully called "worshiping idols." But the beautiful statue in the palanquin is no idol. This morning the brahmin priests performed *prana pratishta* (infusion of life energy) over the statue and the Mother of the Universe graciously entered the plaster image to receive her children's worship. Everyone here feels her blessing energy as she is carried along the road. With incredible delight, I leap out of the auto-rickshaw to join the celebration.

One of the things I love most about India is that I can worship the Goddess freely here, and no one thinks I'm a New Age flake or a feminist with an axe to grind. Sitting down on the grass here and chanting to the World Mother is as natural and appropriate as breathing. There are temples to the Goddess everywhere in India; her image is painted on alley walls, on the sides of devotees' homes, in the entrance to banks. Over the centuries Christian missionaries, Muslim invaders and Communist radicals have done everything in their power to stamp out the worship of the Goddess. They succeeded everywhere in the world—except India. Hindus still cling to the Goddess like little children hanging on to the hem of their mother's skirt.

Many thousands of years ago the Sarasvati River, which the ancient Indians named after the Wisdom Goddess, ran through the Punjab. Geological studies have shown it was five miles across in some locations—easily rivaling the Amazon River in size. It eventually dried up, disappearing completely by 2,000 B.C. It amazes me to realize that over ages so long that one of the largest rivers in earth's geologic history had time to vanish completely, the Goddess Sarasvati has been loved by the Indian people. Great civilizations have flashed in and out of existence, temples were built to Enlil and Marduk and Zeus and Jupiter—and the temples crumbled, yet Sarasvati is still worshiped daily in orthodox Hindu homes today as she was 6,000 years ago.

In remote antiquity, Sarasvati was particularly revered as the Goddess of Speech. We take language so much for granted now (all of us groaned through grammar studies in grade school) that it's hard for us to grasp how much the ancient Indians venerated language. They considered the ability to speak a shakti, a divine power. They believed that the facility to formulate complex concepts and communicate them through sound was a crowning glory of our species. Language was so holy that Panini, India's greatest grammarian, was considered a sage. The power to think, the power to then make one's thoughts known to others, and further still the power to preserve the thoughts of one's ancestors in the form of oral texts like the *Vedas,* handed down by word of mouth generation to generation, and finally the peculiar sensation of triumph when nascent ideas in the mind coalesced into important and original insights—these are all governed by Sarasvati, the Goddess of Wisdom.

The analogy of a river Goddess feels right to me. Writers, musicians, scientists, and philosophers often report they don't "think out" their work; at some moment of its own a solution or poem or melody pours fully formed into their conscious mind. It sweeps them away like a strong current. Interestingly, although geologists say the Sarasvati River disappeared late in the Vedic era, legend claims it continues to flow underground. The confluence of the Ganges, Yamuna and Sarasvati rivers at Prayag is considered so sacred that the Kumbha Mela, Hinduism's most massive festival attended by millions of pilgrims, is still held at this spot every twelve years—even though the Sarasvati is no longer visible! Devotees believe that under the earth the great river continues its secret flow. In a similar manner, the Goddess Sarasvati's divine intelligence runs under the surface of our thoughts until we still our minds so it can bubble to the surface through a hole in our mental chatter. The world's greatest artists, scientists and mystics, according to the Hindus, are those special souls who can sit with total concentration at the Goddess's spring, drinking of its hidden wisdom and creative power.

Of the myriad Indian goddesses, Sarasvati was considered so important that she was called the wife of Brahma, the Creator God himself. She quickly overshadowed her consort however; today there ares only four temples dedicated to Brahma in India while Sarasvati continues to be worshipped in every village. Sarasvati's association with creativity is still close; artists, dancers and musicians consider the white Goddess their personal muse.

The Goddess is also the force of cosmic creativity. While her consort the Creator frames the universe in his mind, it is she who actually manifests it in the form of divine vibrations. Before the beginning was the great water; it was Sarasvati's fingertips which stirred the still lake of undisturbed, unlimited energy into a living stream, sparking suns and causing the clusters of supergalaxies to revolve. Even today she glides over the waves of energy we perceive as the physical universe on her delicate white swan.

"Sarasvati ki jai!" the children are shouting as they throw off their clothes and leap into the river where the crowd has brought the beautiful white statue of the Wisdom Goddess. The priests are chanting mantras as they immerse the Mother; even now her plaster body is dissolving in the water, the river Goddess returning to the river, form returning to the formless. I'm sopping wet but not because I've been swimming. The kids are squirting each other—and me—with water guns; I'm laughing so hard I can hardly stand up.

The schoolchildren honoring her today are just launching into their academic studies, but Sarasvati has more to teach than reading and writing, music and rhetoric. She can unveil the mystical essence of reality itself. Since the human race began she has beckoned the greatest of yogis and yoginis, saints and sages, inviting them into the invisible chambers of the universe.

THE INNER SKY

My favorite story about Sarasvati appears in the 8th century mystical classic, the *Yoga Vasishtha*, one of the longest books ever written and certainly one of the most astonishing. A fourteen-year-old prince named Rama had recently returned from a tour of the surrounding countryside. He experienced the same reaction to the disease, death and poverty he found outside the privileged enclave of his parents' city, that the young Buddha felt when he too first saw the terrible suffering of the mass of humanity. Rama lost all interest in his studies, his girlfriends, sports and politics, and moped alone in his room in a state of mind-numbing depression.

Fortunately, Rama's father retained an exceptionally wise counselor named Vasishtha. Vasishtha was a very advanced yogi who used to spend his spare time visiting other universes or sometimes just completely immersing himself in the pure bliss of limitless awareness. Vasishtha instantly grasped why Rama was so distraught and secretly approved, because awakening to the cruel realities of life is often the first step toward expanded awareness and compassionate service. He sat down with the despondent boy and began to explain why things are the way they are. Because he was speaking to a child, Vasishtha illustrated these teachings in the form of stories. One of these tales was about a queen named Lila and her encounter with the Wisdom Goddess.

Lila had it all: a luxurious life at court and a marvelous and deeply fulfilling marriage. Festering underneath her happiness, however, a canker ached continually in her heart. She knew one day, sooner or later, death would come, and the thought that her husband Padma might die first upset her deeply. She couldn't imagine going on without him. So she began doing spiritual practices, hoping to invoke the grace of Sarasvati.

From the formless realms of infinite knowledge and bliss, the vast consciousness called Sarasvati noted the sincere yearning of the human queen, who sat earnestly before her altar offering flower petals to her statue of the Goddess of Wisdom, chanting the praise of the Goddess, praying, and diving deep into meditation. Sarasvati felt the magnetic pull of Lila's intense devotion and willed to appear before her in human form.

Lila looked up from her meditation seat to find the luminous Goddess, dressed in a radiant white sari with blue and gold trim, smiling down at her. "Be victorious, Mother!" she exclaimed. "You are the glowing moon of compassion that ends our misery here in the world. You are the sun that dispels the darkness of our sorrow!"

"I am deeply pleased with your devotion," Sarasvati laughed. "Now please tell me, how can I help you?" The Goddess's eyes twinkled with delight—she knew exactly what Lila wanted.

"I have two wishes, Mother. The first is that my husband would never die, but I understand that even you cannot grant that boon. So I ask instead that if Padma should pass away before I do, his consciousness remain near me so I can continue enjoying his company for the rest of my life."

"And your second request?"

"Darling Mother, please appear me to every time I call out to you!"

The Goddess's beautiful face shone with love. "As you wish," she smiled, and then the white robed body she had assumed ceased to exist!

The years rolled by and finally one dismal day Padma, old and sick, breathed his last. Lila went into shock, near death herself with grief at the loss of her lifelong companion. Feeling the sorrow of her devotee, Sarasvati was filled with compassion. She reappeared to Lila, bringing relief, the text says, "like a rain shower to dying fish in a drying pond." She instructed the queen to place the body in a sepulcher in her inner compartment and cover it with flowers and herbs.

"Where is Padma now?" Lila desperately wanted to know. "What is he experiencing? Please take me to him!"

"He is roaming in the sky," the Goddess answered. "There are three kinds of sky, Lila. The first is the one you see with your eyes. The second is the sky of your mind, where your thoughts and feelings pass like clouds. The third is the *chid akasha*, the clear blue sky of consciousness which contains the other two. That is where you will find Padma."

Lila sat up straight, shut her eyes, relaxed her body, and concentrated her mind. Withdrawing her awareness from her physical senses, she mentally entered the *chid akasha*. Sure enough, Padma was there, although he now looked much younger. She eased herself into his mental universe to see what he was experiencing. It turned out he was conferring with ambassadors from various parts of India and Sri Lanka. All the usual hubbub of court life was going on around him: priests reciting verses from the sacred *Vedas*, servants rushing about on their errands, horses and elephants making a racket in the courtyard. Lila moved invisibly through the commotion, amazed to see the same hills in the distance that surrounded the court in her own physical world and the same courtiers who waited on her in her court. This seriously alarmed her: had all the members of her court suddenly died and joined Padma in this copy of the external world which he was experiencing in his consciousness? Lila ended her meditation, jumped up and ran out into the courtyard. No—everyone was still here, saddened by the recent loss of their king but healthy nonetheless.

The queen was completely dumbfounded. Here was her world and all its inhabitants, the same as usual. And yet the late king was continuing to experience every nuance of this world in his own mind. He didn't even seem to have noticed that he was dead!

"Sarasvati! Sarasvati!"

The great Goddess graciously responded to Lila's call, once again assuming the white-robed form the queen recognized. Lila brought a comfortable chair for the Goddess and sat down at her feet.

"Mother, it was your wisdom that created this universe, establishing its hidden laws. You know the Truth because you are the Truth. In Padma's consciousness I found an entire world as extensive as my own. I can't understand this! There were even planets and stars following similar orbits in that parallel world. It's hard for me to tell which of the two worlds is actually real!"

Sarasvati looked thoughtful for a moment and then asked, "Tell me, Lila, what do you mean by 'real'?"

"I'm real! I'm sitting here looking at you and that's real! But my husband is dead. He doesn't have a body. He's not in this world. The world he thinks he's perceiving must be a total illusion! What I see going on around me is really happening. What he sees is a fantasy based on memories of his recent life. It's just a shadow in his mind!"

The Goddess appeared amused. "You're right. His world is just a figment in the space of his awareness. However, if we are going to continue your education, there is something more you need to understand. Lila, your world too exists only in your mind. It also is no more than a shadow."

"What?"

"Let me tell you about a brahmin woman named Arundhati. You have quite a bit in common with her. One day her husband was sitting on a hill near their home when he saw a king and his royal retinue pass through the valley. The brahmin found himself envying the king and for years after daydreamed about becoming a great monarch himself, powerful and famous and prosperous and splendid. Ultimately, of course, he died, as miserably poor as ever. His devoted wife appealed to me just as you have, requesting that her husband's soul remain near her forever. Granting her request, I ensured his spirit never left their tiny hut. Yet because of his intense desires, in the sky of his consciousness the brahmin now found himself a great king, learned and respected and a terror to his enemies. Eight days ago Arundhati died and rejoined her husband in the space of his mind. Their intertwined souls remain locked in the confines of their small hut while their awareness ranges in a new life filled with luxury and royalty.

"Lila, *you* are Arundhati. Arundhati was your previous birth. And the brahmin priest was the last life of your husband Padma. Or should I say that Padma, the king whose luxurious lifestyle fulfilled the brahmin's fantasies, was the future incarnation of Arundhati's husband?"

"Mother, this doesn't make sense! You're saying that I—in the form of Arundhati—died only a week ago, yet here I am as Lila, a middle aged woman! You're saying although I experience myself living in opulence in the royal court, in some sense my conscious-ness is still confined to the brahmin couple's hut? I'm sorry, I don't understand!"

The Goddess leaned forward in her chair, tenderly running her fingers through Lila's hair. "My darling daughter, you asked me what is real and what is unreal. Don't you understand yet? From your perspective this royal chamber is real. From Padma's perspective his new kingdom is real. In reality all of this is unreal. All of this is a figment in the universal mind. This globe called the earth and everything it contains exists in one tiny pocket in one small corner of my infinitely vast consciousness. Every individual soul the Creator has imagined into existence contains within itself unnumbered worlds within worlds. Yet the Creator himself is a figment in the all pervading consciousness/energy that is the unchanging reality behind these phenomena. You see yourself as a solid body—you see all this world as solid—but in reality you are almost entirely empty space. You and the universe itself are nothing more than the minutest stirring in the consciousness of the Supreme One.

"You ask how your previous life could have ended only eight days ago. Lila, you take time and space so seriously! In my experience there are no such things as distance or duration. The structure of your mind imposes these ideas on a completely unfettered reality. Brahma the Creator wills into existence the material elements, and all the worlds and all the creatures those elements form. But where did Brahma come from? In what sense does the Creator exist? He himself is a product of my *maya,* my illusory power.

"So you see, from one perspective all these worlds—the one you're experiencing and the ones the souls you imagine have died are experiencing—all these worlds are real. But in my experience they are all dreams, completely insubstantial. My infinite being is all pervading. How can anything finite exist in my unlimited being?

"You are so terribly concerned about your husband, so let me explain what happens to a person after death. The outer world vanishes when his senses fail but he remembers his entire previous life, his friends and family, his failures and successes. His entire life flashes before his eyes in a split second—he sees seventy years in one instant because he is no longer limited by space and time—but he does not remain in this state for long. Soon the infinitesimal sphere of his awareness assumes another body as transparent as the air but which seems corporeal to him. He lives out another life from infancy to old age, and as death once again encroaches he feels a peculiar sensation that it has all been a dream, that a hundred years rushed by in a moment. Then he passes away from that reality into yet another self-created world. All the self-created worlds of all the souls are held in place in the self-created universe of Brahma.

"Lila, my point is this. This tangible world rests in the intangible spirit of Divine Being—much like pungency inheres in pepper! Ah, Lila, I have given eyes to many creatures but few are the clear-sighted beings who see into the true nature of things!

"Ultimately time, space and causality are nothing more than empty words. True wisdom consists in knowing me as I truly am— unbounded universal intelligence. The finite events you experience have no reality apart from your own intelligence. And you have no reality apart from me."

Lila was reeling. "Divine Mother, this glimpse into your wisdom-consciousness is like peering into blazing lightning with unshielded eyes! Please help me understand these abstract truths by showing me concrete examples. I want to go to the hut where my previous self, Arundhati, recently died."

Smiling, the Goddess replied, "Lila, spiritual vision is greatly hampered by the physical body. Through the practice of yoga you can purify yourself to the point where conditioning beliefs such as 'I am my body and therefore I cannot travel unless my body moves through space' are removed. You must find the place inside yourself that exists beyond thought, and learn to fly through the inner sky. Then your physical eyes will no longer offer any obstruction to your power of sight.

"When your mind subsides into its pure essence, undistracted by random thoughts and desires, it glows and begins to flow. When the structure imposed on your consciousness by your sense of egotism is loosened, spontaneously you will begin to perceive beings and events that are invisible to you now. You will look into other worlds and discover aspects of reality that are presently utterly beyond your imagination.

"You want to visit the brahmins' former home. Close your eyes, still your mind, and let's go."

Linking their minds in an immaterial union, the queen and the Goddess rose into the sky. Soaring through the atmosphere in a body made of pure awareness, Lila noted the many beings who live above the earth: the *siddhas* or perfect yoga masters who perform their meditation in the heavens, other entities whose bodies are composed of sound or light, and malicious energies looking for weak-willed humans to feed from. As meteors flared past her, Lila looked down on the glacier swathed Himalayas, glittering in the sunlight as if they were on fire.

Sarasvati carried Lila higher so that she could actually see part of the orb of the earth in the shadow of night, and watch as the boundary of daylight slipped across the face of the planet. She saw vast tracts of weather moving over the continents. Some land masses were covered with clouds; others she could make out distinctly through the clear air. Lila could distinguish the lush green tropics from the glittering white poles as well as the enormous oceans that covered most of her home world.

Glancing upward, the queen saw the great white band of the Milky Way and several of the planets of our solar system. And beyond, looming cold and empty, was the limitless vacuum of space.

Then the two etherial beings alighted in the former home of the brahmin pair, where relatives were still grieving over the recent deaths of Arundhati and her husband. A middle aged man rushed forward to greet them, scattering flower petals at their feet. "Victory to you, compassionate goddesses! You must have come to relieve us of our sorrow with the blessing of this vision of your luminous forms!"

Lila instantly intuitively recognized the man as her eldest son Jyestha in her previous/simultaneous incarnation as the brahmin wife Arundhati. Leaning forward, Lila gently touched his forehead with her fingertips, and immediately his deep sense of loss at the death of his parents vanished.

As they rose back into the air, Lila turned to Sarasvati with another question. "When I visited Padma's world after his death, no one saw me. How is it that Jyestha was able to see me?"

"During your first trip out of your body, you still partially clung to your sense of selfhood. You were acting on behalf of your self-centered desire to see your husband; your yoga was not perfect. This time you let go of yourself enough to surrender totally to the process of mental travel. When you saw your former son you did not think of yourself but wanted only to relieve his pain. The purity of your motivation made it possible for you to contact him. Your pure love was visible to him."

"Thank you, Mother, for fulfilling my desire to visit this place. Indeed I feel an eerie sense of recognition about that house, that hill, that whole region, as if I actually did live there. But I have one more desire I beg you to fulfill. Please take me to my husband!"

The Goddess laughed out loud. "You'll have to be more specific! Lila, which husband of yours do you want to see? You've had dozens you know, both in the past and the future. There are at least three on this planet right now."

"*What?*"

"There is the brahmin priest whose center of consciousness is still in the house below us. There is king Padma whose center of consciousness is still in your chamber in the palace. And there is a third one who is a powerful prince reigning on the earth at this very moment. I'll tell you frankly he's a rather stupid fellow, very puffed up with himself, dwelling constantly on how large his kingdom is and how wealthy he is. He doesn't even realize the terrible danger he's in. Now which of these husbands would you like to visit?

"Don't look so surprised, dear. You mustn't forget that although all this is real, none of it is real. Those stars in the sky—they look so close don't they? You feel you could almost reach up and catch one. It's an illusion; in reality they're all millions of miles away. The people we see below us are illusions too, empty space on which our minds project bodies and personalities. They are really just the sparest collections of atoms, tiny particles as far apart from each other comparatively as the stars are from one another, no more tangible than sunbeams. Lila, all the atoms in this universe can be compressed into a ball no larger than a handful of rice. To those who look only with their physical eyes, the vast vault of the night sky looks like a tapestry of shimmering jewels. Those who look with the eyes of the soul see only the glory of God."

Sarasvati tenderly stroked Lila's face. "You have been married many times. Remember?"

Lila's eyes widened with astonishment. "I do remember! Yes I remember! I remember being projected from the mind of the Creator, undergoing a hundred—no—a hundred and eight births, and here I am, still in existence!

"Yes I do remember this husband, the arrogant king you speak of. His name is Viduratha. He and I devoted our lives to the pursuit of pleasure. I loved him very much.

"I remember I lived as a young woman in the forest once, and died and experienced myself as a plant growing in that same forest. There was a wildfire and I burned away. Then I was born as the daughter of a recluse practicing yoga in the woods. He taught me to meditate. But I wanted to be a male because I thought then I'd have more freedom, so I came back as a prince named Surat. I was absolutely awful, a bully! After that I was born as a weasel, horribly diseased, because of my terrible behavior in the previous life.

"I remember being a bullock, and how much it hurt when the herders hit me with their sticks. I was a bird too, and remember how hard it was to break free from the net when a hunter trapped me. I was a fish once, and remember seeing a man bludgeon a turtle to death. He couldn't break its shell so he hit it on the neck. Once I was a fairy and lived in the flowers. I thought I was so beautiful!

"I remember being a girl again, flirting with young men and purposely breaking their hearts. And then I remember, so vividly, a lonely lifetime, lying alone in bed. I longed so much for a man, but none would have me.

"Yes I remember them all, all my lifetimes! So much pain, so much longing!

"I remember my life as Arundhati in great detail. I was always so busy—there was no time for yoga or philosophy! I was cleaning the house, fetching water, milking the cows, churning butter. I collected fuel and cooked and cooked and cooked. I had baby after baby. I was so thin and sick. I wrapped myself in a threadbare blanket. Oh look below! There's my—I mean Arundhati's—pet calf Karnika! Amazing—even though I haven't been there to chase her away in over a week, she's been behaving! She hasn't been nibbling on the vegetables I—I mean Arundhati—planted!

"And there he is, my husband from that lifetime! All his life he fantasized about becoming a great king and look now, he imagines he's Viduratha and he rules a large kingdom! Let's visit his capital city. I'd like to see it from the air!" Lila bowed to the Goddess, then leapt into the sky like a bird.

In her enthusiasm for flight, Lila passed not only the clouds and rivers of air in the upper atmosphere, but the orbit of the moon. In less than the amount of time it takes to think the words, she sailed past the pole star and through the Milky Way. She lost sight of the sun when its rays were blocked by a dark nebula. When she spotted it again it was no larger than an atom, almost lost amongst the innumerable stars in the vastnesses of space.

Outer space amazed Lila. There was no beginning, middle or end to the vacuum: it was an infinite expanse serenely resting in Divine Spirit. If a phoenix, fast as thought itself, should try to fly from one end to the other, Lila reflected, even if it flew as rapidly as it possibly could, in eons and eons and eons it would not come to the end of the limitless space the Divine Intelligence effortlessly held in its awareness.

From far out in the infinitude, Lila looked back on her universe. It looked like a great, translucent egg filled with billions and billions of sparkling particles called stars, all in motion. There was no way to determine which direction was up or down—everything danced around everything else. Lila observed that some masses of matter were clumping together forming new worlds, while others were breaking apart, dwindling into ineffable nothingness. A lot of the worlds were surrounded by bracelet-like rings. Many of them were populated, some with human-like beings, others with stone-like or plant-like intelligences, and some with beings so strange that even yogis can't understand what they are!

Shifting through the space of her awareness, Lila returned to her palace and sat down beside her husband's coffin. Then focusing intently, she re-entered the sky of Padma's consciousness. The scenes playing before his mind were gruesome. Earlier in his manifestation as the brahmin priest, Padma had desired to become a king. Taking birth as Padma he had the opportunity to fulfill his desires for power and fame but instead life at court had fanned the flame of his lusts, and he found himself desiring more land and greater military power. After Padma's death he began living out the life of king Viduratha and now the inevitable consequences of his greed were coming to pass. King Sindhu was attacking with an enormous army. Viduratha was at war, desperately trying to protect his land and his subjects. The fighting was bitter but called forth all the valor in Viduratha's heart. He and his soldiers fought fiercely but the carnage was awesome. The sun had not yet set before animal scavengers were slinking into the battlefield, gorging on the dead and dying.

As night settled over the grim landscape, Viduratha returned to his tent to rest. Lila and Sarasvati assumed visible bodies and slipped into the tent through a tiny tear in the fabric.

HIDDEN PASSAGEWAYS

At this point young prince Rama interrupted the narrative. "Wait a minute, Vasishtha! If Lila and the Goddess are in material bodies now, how could they pass through a small hole?"

The aged counsellor sighed. "If anyone believes they really have a physical body, there is no way they could fit through a hole tinier than a fingernail. But if you understand that although your body is a cage, you are in no way obstructed by it—if you understand that although your body can easily be measured, your spirit has no circumference whatsoever, then whenever you wish to go anywhere, passageways will instantly appear. Identify your consciousness with your body and you are limited to your body. Identify your body with your consciousness and your body becomes as free as thought itself. Just as cold air sinks while flames leap upward, so it is the tendency of the material body to sink downwards and of the spirit to rise. Your inner intelligence can move in either direction, however, depending on how you train it.

"You know, of course, that all living things have a subtle body. You can feel its presence within you when you pay close attention. Yogis and yoginis move about in this immaterial form when carrying their physical body along is too much of a nuisance. Advanced masters can materialize a duplicate physical body when they get where they're going, if they need to. Occasionally they meet people so obtuse that the yogis can't get their attention or communicate with them at all unless they wear a physical body, so this skill comes in handy.

"But there's another point you should be clear about. My boy, consciousness, mind and space: these are not three different things. Each of these is all pervading. The true intelligence inside you, the awareness buried beneath the everyday rambling of your mind, pervades all of space. It encompasses every atom in the universe.

It encompasses every galaxy. All living beings are connected through this network of intelligence. It is the basis of telepathy, precognition, and the other occult powers.

"This intelligence is perfectly tranquil, which is why people with agitated minds are unable to tap into it. It existed before the creation of the universe and comprehends the nature of all things. That is how, even though in our era we have few scientific instruments, we yogis can accurately describe what the earth looks like from the moon, the character of our galaxy, and the death of stars.

"My dear boy, today we worship great gods like Brahma, Vishnu and Shiva. In reality there have been untold millions and billions of such gods throughout the course of the existence of innumerable universes appearing and disappearing in the expanse of the Divine Intelligence. There is a part of your mind—I know you sense it at times—that dwells within this Divine Intelligence. Yogis call it the unconfined body. It is present everywhere and its powers are unlimited.

"Ah, Rama, this world is all unreal. Unreal, that is, in the sense that you understand reality. Yet at the same time it is the seat of the Supreme Consciousness and I find it very, very interesting. But let's resume our story."

WHO ARE YOU?

The king was astonished at the two fairy-like forms which appeared in his tent and leapt up to greet them. He wanted to ask them who they were but instead the Goddess asked him who he was. "I am Viduratha, the son of Naghoratha of the Ikshaku imperial line. I am lord of all this region you see!"

"Are you really?" Sarasvati smiled. She placed her fingers on his head and instantly the veil of his identity fell away.

"Goddess, I see everything now! Seventy years of this life have passed and yet it is only one day since I last died—my name was Padma and the woman standing beside you is—was—Lila, my deeply cherished wife. Before that I was a priest who used to sit in the hills daydreaming about becoming a king! And there were many more lives before that. They go on and on!"

"Yes, you can see now that your present life is just a shadow cast by your former existence. The current of the mind is a wave that rolls across the sea of the Universal Intelligence, rising in life, ebbing in death. And yet the reality is that you never died, nor have you ever been born. The Self within you has watched all these lifetimes come and go like dreams. Turn back to that Self inside you and you will find you are not Viduratha the son of Naghoratha, but an immortal and unlimited intelligence more vast than the cosmos itself.

"There is one more thing I need to tell you," the Goddess continued. "Today you are going to die. You will fall in battle and your city will be destroyed. But your former wife standing here beside me has won my favor, and for her sake I will carry you back to Padma's corpse which she has carefully preserved. You will re-enter your previous body and resume your royal destiny. But first you have business to attend to." Sarasvati waved toward the tent door.

At that instant horse hooves thundered up outside and a frantic messenger burst into the tent. "Sir! The city is in flames! Sindhu's army set upon us in the night. We are vastly outnumbered!"

Viduratha sprang out of the tent to behold the most blood curdling sight he had seen in his long, violent career. His beloved city was burning to the ground, being sacked by frenzied looters. Whole families trapped inside their homes were screaming as they burned to death. The merciless invaders were killing every man who managed to escape a flaming building and savagely assaulting the surviving women. Helpless children were being hacked to pieces. This was a scene that had repeated itself thousands of times in history, but now it was his own people being put to the sword. Viduratha shrieked in rage.

At that moment another retreating party rushed into the camp and Viduratha turned to see his terrified wife running toward him. Lila stepped back in shock. It was herself—a perfect mirror image of Lila throwing herself into Viduratha's arms. "How can this be?" she gasped to Sarasvati.

"Padma loved you very much," the Goddess answered, "and carried this image of you with him into his new existence. Oh yes, she's alive—she really is you. Although, in another sense, she's no more real than you are. Remember that everything that exists is merely a ray emanating from the consciousness of the Supreme One. Living beings refract this ray in their own minds like prisms, and so colors and sounds and smells appear to them as real when all they are in fact are subtle vibrations in Divine Awareness. Even the absolute horror you see in the valley below us is ultimately nothing more than waves in a divine sea of consciousness and energy. Can you grasp this, Lila?"

Viduratha was already reaching for his horse and moments later was thundering into battle with his troops. Viduratha's wife cried for joy when she saw him beat back the onslaught, and wept with terror as the enemy regrouped and pushed the king's forces back.

Lila felt strangely tranquil. Earlier in her life she could not have borne to watch this scene but now she had the odd sense that it was all a dream. Warriors, revelling in brutality, had called this holocaust into existence. Innocent citizens, blindly clinging to their possessions as if they were theirs to keep forever, were seeing the transient things of the world torn away from them. It was awful beyond imagination, yet Lila found herself literally abiding beyond imagination in the tranquil haven of her soul. How strange to feel such deep peace, even here amidst this savagery! And yet she had always known this peace; it had always existed at the core of her being. It existed everywhere, even in the flaming city below.

Viduratha's wife collapsed when she saw her husband's neck severed by an enemy sword. "The sky of her consciousness is one with the sky of Viduratha's awareness," Sarasvati explained. "The shock of seeing her beloved die has killed her, and even now the essence of her being is merging with his.

"Look now at how arrogantly the victorious king Sindhu marches through the pillaged city! When he was young he worshipped me sincerely; this is what gave him the strength to conquer his enemy. But just see his behavior now! His cruelty and rapacity have cut him off from my wisdom and inspiration entirely. That is why although I am the Goddess to whom he was once so devoted, he cannot see me standing here now so close by, even though all he would have to do is turn his head."

Lila turned to face Sarasvati. "Oh Mother, so many people have been killed! Tell me the truth about death: is it painful? Or is it a beautiful experience, as others claim?"

"The truth is that it varies from person to person. There are some people absolutely convinced there is no life after death; I have seen them remain completely unconscious for as long as a year after they die. They simply don't believe they're going to wake up!

"Those who are advanced in meditation have no problem at death at all. They remain alert throughout the process and go wherever they wish after leaving their bodies. During their lives they learned to withdraw their awareness from their physical senses and made themselves at home in the inner worlds. Each time they sat down and meditated was, in effect, a dress rehearsal for death.

"I'm afraid the story is not so happy for those who have never devoted themselves to spiritual life. Death catches them completely unprepared. I will tell you frankly that for them the experience is often horrendous, filled with fear and confusion.

"People who have lived decent lives, have served others and have sincerely practiced their religious faiths, will be briefly disoriented after death but will soon find themselves in the heavens to which they expect to go. Their stay there will be pleasant and serene. But ultimately the tug of their unfulfilled desires will pull them back into whatever type of material body is most likely to allow them to satisfy their cravings.

"Ultimately death, like life, is an illusion. If you believe you are your body, life is serious for you and death is all too real. However, if you understand that your body is only one small part of the infinitude of your being, life becomes a child's game and death a change of clothes. But you can't just know this intellectually or accept it on faith. You must experience it directly by penetrating beyond the limits imposed on your consciousness by your senses. Then your tiny reality expands into a much greater reality and you personally experience the sacredness of every atom in the universe, as well as your perfect unity with all other living beings.

"Lila, all the animate creatures you see around you are in fact physical projections of their own thoughts. As it imagines itself, so the soul becomes. The mind which abides in Divine Awareness however, remaining self-composed and unshaken by the vagaries of external events, experiences complete spiritual emancipation when the body it has projected fades away. Unfortunately it's very difficult to maintain this level of awareness when the pushes and pulls of life, the pleasures and aggravations that play across the screen of the Creator God's consciousness, continually impinge on your senses. It requires tremendous focus to redirect the mind toward the eternal reality behind the flickering chimera of external phenomena like people and events and your own meandering train of thoughts.

"When you recognize and experience yourself to be the one who measures the passage of time, the objects shifting their positions as the past gives way to the future, and the very force of time itself, then time and causality will no longer dictate your perceptions. There is only one Being which, although it appears in the forms of sunlight and darkness, in fact never rises or sets anywhere. It has no beginning, middle or end, but is like a limitless expanse of water. When we are no longer caught in its currents, when we no longer helplessly bob on the surface of its waves, then we realize that we are ourselves that ocean of unlimited Being. Discover your true nature, Lila. Bathe in the ocean of all pervading awareness lapping at the banks of your personality."

"Oh Mother," Lila cried out in awe, "may it be so! And yet even now I feel the tug of my karma pulling me back to fulfill my obligations in my world. I think I should return to my body and live out my life, performing my duties while continuing to immerse myself in the sea of your wisdom."

The Goddess's lovely white teeth glistened like polished pearls as she laughed. "I'm afraid you can't do that. Your body has just been cremated."

"What?"

"This short journey of ours that seemed to us to take only moments corresponded to over a month in your physical world. The maids found you lying unbreathing in your room. They concluded you must have killed yourself in grief over Padma's death. So they took your body to the cremation grounds and burned it.

"But don't worry. This new, purer body of yours will do just as nicely. It even looks enough like your old self so that your subjects will be able to recognize you."

Lila and Sarasvati projected themselves back to Padma's body, still lying perfectly preserved under its blanket of flowers and herbs in Lila's inner chamber. Sarasvati swept the flowers away with one graceful gesture of her hand, leaned over the corpse, and breathed into Padma's nostrils. Her *prana,* her life energy, infused his form. Slowly one portion of his body after another grew warm and supple, and finally the dazed king sat up in his petal-strewn bed. "What happened?" he asked in bewilderment. "I was having the strangest dream!"

"Darling," Lila fumbled to explain, "your illness was more serious than we thought. I'm afraid you died, dear. The woman standing next to you is Sarasvati, the Goddess of Wisdom and Mother of the Worlds. Out of her extraordinary grace she has brought you back to me."

Padma leapt out of bed and threw himself at Sarasvati's feet. Then he jumped up and rushed to fetch a chair gilded with gold for the Goddess to sit on. "Divine Mother," he cried out, "it is a blessing beyond measure to receive this vision of you! Please also bless my wife and me with understanding, wealth and long life!"

The Goddess's eyes glowed with love like a mother watching her innocent child at play. Grazing Padma's forehead with her fingertips she whispered, "May you never be disturbed by evil events or by evil thoughts. May no misfortune enter this palace, may delight flourish perpetually in your heart, and may the people of your kingdom be safe, happy and prosperous. Let all joys attend you forever."

Padma threw his arms around his devoted wife and as the reunited couple embraced, the smiling Goddess gradually faded from view.

Lila and Padma reigned for many years. Under their inspired guidance the kingdom became a stronghold of wisdom, virtue and joy. Many great yoga masters came to visit the pair, to teach them and be taught by them. When they died, Lila and Padma merged their joint essence into the Divine Intelligence, propelled by the radiant wisdom energy of the white robed Goddess who shimmered continually in their grateful hearts.

The old priest Vasishtha sat with Rama for days, telling him story after story about great yogis and yoginis, and recounting his own adventures and the many extraordinary creatures he had encountered as he himself travelled between universes. Rama was completely enthralled. "Now I understand, Vasishtha! Although the world is filled with terrible suffering, none of it is really real. So I shouldn't worry about it anymore!"

The old man roared with laughter. "My dear boy, if that is what you've understood, then you haven't understood anything at all! Remember that although from the perspective of your Highest Self, the entire universe with all its joy and sorrow is just a play of vibrations across the screen of Divine Awareness, from the point of view of the finite beings within these worlds, joy and sorrow are all too real. The Divine Mother didn't place us here to just sit back and enjoy the show. We were given the experience of finitehood so that we can engage in the world process. Within the Creator's dream, we all have roles to play, and conscientiously fulfilling our responsibilities is our most solemn duty.

"Rama, it is your destiny to become a great king. Therefore it is your sacred responsibility to protect and defend your subjects, to provide for the poor and the sick, to nurture religion and the arts, and to set an example for all your people of how to live each moment with honesty and integrity. The Goddess doesn't reveal her innermost secrets for our intellectual satisfaction alone; she does so so that we can put aside our despair and take an active role in improving conditions in the world, grounding our actions in wisdom and compassion. Therefore, my boy, wherever you find pain or injustice, act at once to correct it, but do not allow yourself to give in to anger or depression when the task appears overwhelming. Remember that the deepest essence of your being is more vast than the universe itself, and return again and again to that infinite resource within you for guidance and inspiration. Remember that the Divine Mother is closer to you than your own thoughts, and will foster everything that is best in you throughout life, death and beyond.

"Now we've been sitting chattering here for days on end like naughty truants. Aren't you supposed to be in school? You have a long life of public service ahead of you. Shouldn't you be preparing yourself?"

Prince Rama grinned, bowed to the old priest, and ran out to his classroom where, with the loving blessing of Goddess Sarasvati, his fellow students were beginning their day's studies.

THE GODDESS ON THE WHITE SWAN

As traffic begins to edge forward, I climb back into the auto-rickshaw. Sitting back in the cab in a dusty village in Bihar, listening to Sarasvati's name shouted again and again by ecstatic devotees, I can't help wishing the Goddess would appear to me as she did to Lila. From the dawn of history up through this very moment sincere Hindus have been propitiating her. Many invoke her with hymns like the *Sarasvati Rahasya Upanishad,* the sacred scripture I've quoted at the end of this chapter. By focusing on her form and attributes, and by chanting the special mantras included with the text, devotees call the Goddess and her attendant blessings into their lives.

For some worshipers, Sarasvati is as real as their own mother. To them she may appear in physical form, gracing their lives with her wisdom teachings as she did with Lila. Most Westerners find it hard to believe that a Goddess could actually materialize out of the ether at the call of a sincere devotee, though I will leave it to them to explain how the *Yoga Vasishtha's* description of the earth from outer space could be accurate in almost every detail and reminiscent of film footage taken by astronauts from the Space Shuttle, or how it could offer such an astonishingly prescient knowledge of atomic theory. Remember, the *Yoga Vasishtha* was composed in India 1,300 years ago. If the author wasn't getting his or her advanced knowledge of astronomy and molecular science from Sarasvati, where did it come from?

Others may never actually see the Goddess with their eyes, but they concretely experience her blessings and inspiration. The greatest musicians will confess that when they are playing their best, although their hands tender the instrument, it is Sarasvati who is strumming it. Teachers relate that when Sarasvati blesses their power of speech, they see their students' eyes light up with the excitement of inspired understanding. She is the actual teacher though they are the vehicle for the teaching; she is also the power of comprehension in the minds of the pupils.

There are still others for whom Sarasvati is as close as their own Self. These are the blessed ones who recite the *Sarasvati Rahasya Upanishad,* "The Secret Knowledge of the Wisdom Goddess," and truly grasp its import. Ultimately the Wisdom Goddess does not exist outside ourselves, nor we outside of her. Perhaps when we truly understand who and what Sarasvati is, we will for the first time truly understand what we are ourselves.

Here is one of the classical hymns with which the yogis and yoginis invoke Sarasvati. The verses are from the *Rig Veda;* they are more than 4,000 years old. Following these stanzas the Goddess herself speaks. She has one final, extremely important secret she would like to share with all of us. I think you'll find it compelling.

Sarasvati Rahasya Upanishad:

THE SECRET KNOWLEDGE
OF THE WISDOM GODDESS

With loving reverence I bow to the Goddess Sarasvati, who is pure and luminous as snow, as pearl, as camphor and the bright full moon, who with great delight bountifully bestows her gracious blessings, who is adorned with fragrant golden flower petals, and whose beautiful form captivates my enraptured mind.

She whose nature is the essence of truth,
　　she is the Universal Empress
　　appearing as all things and as their names.
Sarasvati: Bestow your abundant blessing!
May Goddess Sarasvati
　　who nourishes our minds and souls,
　　who is the guardian of our innermost being,
　　protect all of us forever!

The one reality all scriptures praise,
　　the limitless strength of perfect being,
　　may she, the divine Sarasvati, bless me!
May the sacred, resplendent Sarasvati descend
　　from heaven, from the vastnesses of space,
　　to this, my mental sacrifice.
Hearing my loving call, may the queen of the inner sea
　　be pleased with these simple words!

Goddess of Wisdom, who appears as syllables,
    words, sentences and understanding,
Goddess in whom all meaning inheres
    from beginningless time, grant me your grace!
Goddess who purifies and enriches the soul,
    you who are the treasurer of intelligence,
    please accept these words, my humble offering!

In my own heart, in the heart of the gods,
    you, the Goddess of Wisdom, joyfully reside,
    revealing yourself as inspired speech.
Oh Goddess, increase my understanding!
You who call forth truthful words
    and awaken the nobility in our minds,
    to you we offer our heartfelt worship!

She controls the worlds from within the heart,
    from within the gods, from within the stars.
May that inner Sovereign grant me her abounding grace!
    Sarasvati shines resplendently
    over the vast waters of the universal intelligence,
    radiating insight and creative impulse
    to the reflective mind!

The sages seek her at the root
    of their creative intelligence.
All pervading, unitary, self-aware,
Sarasvati, make me like yourself!
There is the spoken word, the thought,
    the subtle vibration of intent—and silence.
The first is shared, the other three
    are hidden in the inner sanctuary.

She is conceived as all the categories of things
    yet she herself is the One beyond.
Sarasvati, grant me intelligence, understanding,
    and the ability to express myself perfectly, as you do!
She appears as words though she herself is silent,

level after level of meaning
pouring from her in a torrent of partial truths:
energy streams of limited awareness.
Sarasvati, reveal yourself as you really are!

When the articulate—and the inarticulate—speak,
    it is your power that flows.
You are like a cow ever yielding milk
    that fulfills all desires.
Sarasvati, fulfill mine!
When the gods speak, even when animals speak,
    it is your power that flows.
Your milk is so sweet and yet gives us such strength;
    may it flow through us as inner wisdom
    and uplifting words!

Knowing you, we cannot know bondage
    so we hasten along our many paths
    to your one abode.
Protect us on our journey!
Everyone sees but few see you,
    everyone hears but few hear you.
To your earnest supplicant you reveal yourself
    like a loving wife displaying herself
    to her devoted husband.

All things, all languages, arise from you
    and immerse themselves again in you.
Meditating thus, we visualize you
    as supreme, formless being.
Sarasvati, may we remain immersed in you!
Divine Mother! Ever flowing river of divine awareness,
We praise you, supreme consciousness and creative force!
Our praise is not worth much for no one honors us
    till we are honored by you.

You are the swan gliding over the pond of creative energy,
    waves and waves of creative force emanating from your form!

Radiant Goddess, resplendent in white,
     relax and enjoy yourself here in my worshipful mind!

Lying prostrate before you, Goddess of light—
     you who dwell in the Kashmir of my heart—
I beg of you, grant me knowledge and wisdom!
Let me peer with unlimited vision into your undivided heart!

You who hold in your four hands the rosary
     on which you repeat the sacred syllables
     which form the basis of all language,
     the book in which the story of all life is written,
     the goad with which you drive us to yourself, and
     the noose with which you draw us, when we struggle, home,
     you who wear the necklace of immaculate pearls—
     all the shimmering souls in the worlds—
     dwell in my mind and my heart and my speech
     forever, Sarasvati!

Your throat is white and perfect as the conch,
     your smiling lips are red and lovely, the source of all speech.
Please take your seat, great Goddess,
     on my tongue; use it to praise yourself!

You are faith, intelligence, understanding,
Goddess of speech, consort of the Creator.
Your home is in the self-expression of devout souls.
You bestow virtues like control of the mind.

I offer my loving homage to you, Supreme Goddess,
     whose beautiful hair tumbles from your face
     which shines like the moon.
You are the stream of cool nectar which quenches the thirst
     of parched souls wandering in the sorrowful desert of life.

On the devotee who recites these verses with love and faith,
     joyously and without fail worshiping
     the Goddess of perfect silence,

Sarasvati bestows pleasure, artistic skill, knowledge and liberation
   in six short months; there is no doubt!
Through that pure hearted devotee the Goddess will pour
      limitless gifts of inspiration,
      words both beautiful and true.
One knows the essence of all books of wisdom
      without having read a word,
      when one submerges oneself in the ocean
      of Sarasvati's wisdom.

Sarasvati responds:

It was through me the Creator himself
      gained liberating knowledge.
I am being, consciousness, bliss, eternal freedom:
      unsullied, unlimited, unending.

My perfect consciousness shines in your world
      like a beautiful face in a soiled mirror.
Seeing that reflection I call myself you—an individual soul—
      as if I could be finite!

A finite soul, an infinite Goddess—
      these are false concepts in the minds of those
      unacquainted with truth.
No space, my loving devotee,
      exists between your Self and my Self.
Know this and you are free.
This is the secret wisdom.

3

Lakshmi
The Goddess as Wealth and Good Fortune

I am standing outside the Vishnu Pad temple near Gaya in North India. All I can think is, "Sita stood here! Thousands of years ago, she stood at this very spot!" According to legend, one of the greatest heroines of Indian history actually visited this temple.

The site is desolate yet staggeringly beautiful, the atmosphere uncanny. The *mandap*, a wall-less hall whose roof is still held high by cracked pillars, is so ancient that some parts of the stone floor have sunk several feet as the earth shifted over the millennia. I run my fingers across a rock monument on which a message for posterity was inscribed in such vast antiquity that Indian scholars have long since forgotten how to read its weathered script.

At one side of the temple complex the plateau falls away and pilgrims must clamber down extremely deep, steep stairs cut out of the cliff to the dry river bed below. I watch in total amazement as cows serenely make their way down stone steps so perilous I hesitate to try them myself. The Goddess herself must be tending these cows; how else can they survive the descent? When they finally reach the ground thirty feet below, the reason for their exertions becomes clear. They paw in the dry bed till water wells up beneath their hooves and then lean forward to drink.

What did Sita see as she stood peering out over the same vista I'm looking at now? In her era the river bed was host to rushing waters nurturing a thick forest in the desert stretching out before me today. Were the brahmin priests who officiated here thousands of years before the birth of Christ more enlightened than the ones we meet here today, who scramble after every visitor demanding money? Legend says that as she stood here Sita sighed, "Brahmins will always be beggars," and sure enough, her words came true.

Sita was the foster daughter of Janaka, India's equivalent of King Solomon, a ruler of unsurpassed wisdom. One day the childless king was ritually plowing a field to inaugurate the agricultural season, when he uncovered a living infant in the furrow. Honoring tiny Sita as a gift from the Earth Goddess, Janaka joyfully took the baby home and raised her as his own.

In those days when a king wanted to find a suitable husband for his daughter, he'd sponsor a festival filled with contests at which unmarried princes from neighboring kingdoms could come and show off their skills. The princess would then select the young man she liked best. Sita happily chose Rama, the prince of Ayodhya, whose virtue, intelligence, athletic skill and magnetic charm captivated her completely.

In the course of time, however, due to the political machinations of his stepmother, Rama was cheated of the throne and banished to the dark and dangerous forests of prehistoric northern India. Rama accepted his misfortune with cheerful serenity. (When he was a boy, you may recall, an old priest named Vasishtha had taught Rama how to draw on his Higher Self to face any circumstances in life with equanimity and humor.) Sita abandoned the luxuries of life in the palace to voluntarily accompany her husband into the jungle. The couple's many adventures are chronicled in one of the greatest epics in world literature, the *Ramayana*.

Hindus believe that Rama and Sita were real people, and that they lived many, many thousands of years ago. At that time the face of the Earth was quite different than it is today, and it was practically possible to cross from the southern tip of India to Sri Lanka on foot. In that era a surprisingly technologically advanced civilization flourished on Sri Lanka, but it was governed by a rapacious tyrant named Ravanna. Ravanna frequently sent his troops into India to kill and plunder, terrorizing the population with sophisticated weaponry.

Western historians claim it is impossible such an advanced culture could have flourished in Sri Lanka so long ago. Hindus however, like the ancient Egyptians, Greeks, Chaldeans, Aztecs and Hopi, insist that many great nations had already come and gone long before Sumer (which Western scholars believe is the world's oldest civilization) was even born.

To make a very, very long story very, very short, Sita was abducted by Ravanna, who offered enormous wealth and political power in exchange for her love. But even when Ravanna threatened to kill her, Sita remained faithful to her husband. Against unimaginable odds, Rama ultimately rescued his wife.

Every story in India has multiple tiers of meaning, and one way to understand this tale is to see Sita as the human soul, captured by the overpowering forces of the material world, yet never able to forget her divine beloved. If the soul remains firmly devoted to God, refusing to surrender to the temptations of lust, greed and power, the Lord will appear and carry her back to his bed chamber. God loves the soul passionately, as Rama loves Sita.

In every corner of Hindu India, Sita is believed to have been a human incarnation of the Goddess Lakshmi. In the *Sita Upanishad,* the gods, having listened to the story of the *Ramayana,* turn to the Creator God Brahma and ask, "Who, really, is Sita?"

Brahma replies:

She is all creation, and the gods of creation.

She is cause and effect, saints and demons, the elements, souls.

She is supreme virtue and supreme beauty.

The worlds are illuminated by her form as the sun;
    she adorns herself with lightning.

She is the revolving wheel of the cycles of time—
    merely by opening her eyes
    she calls the worlds into being.

As her beautiful eyelids flutter closed
    the universe collapses.

She is the power of enjoyment, the tree of plenty,
    the wish fulfilling gem.

In two hands she bears fragrant lotuses,
    another hand signals the granting of boons,
    while the fourth hand gestures, "Don't be afraid."

She is the Goddess Lakshmi, seated in yoga posture
    on her lion throne.

All the beauty you see around you
    is hers alone, yes, hers alone.

In Indian temples statues of Lakshmi, the Goddess of Good Fortune, are most often seen standing next to her divine consort, Lord Vishnu. He is the immensely popular hero God who protects and sustains the universe, and who incarnated on earth as Sita's husband Rama. While Vishnu and his various incarnations are incredibly popular, in Indian family shrines and businesses pictures of Lakshmi often hold the place of honor. Vishnu is compassionate, but he tempers his blessings with a sense of justice. He rewards us according to our deserts. If it is our karma to suffer, we should suffer—it is his job to maintain order in the universe so he makes sure all debts are paid. But Lakshmi's love is unconditional like a mother's. She forgives instantly. Generosity is her very nature. When Rama attacked Ravanna's capital city, the vicious jailers who had been guarding Sita pleaded with her for forgiveness. When Rama's troops broke through, Sita refused to allow them to harm her captors, even though they had tormented her mercilessly.

In Hindu iconography Lakshmi is usually shown in a red sari, seated or standing on a pink lotus. Often she is holding lotuses in several of her four hands. Sometimes gold coins stream from her palms. She is extraordinarily beautiful. Auspicious white elephants gently shower her with a refreshing spray of cool water.

Let me add here that although multi-limbed deities are disconcerting to Western eyes, these images make perfect sense to many Eastern peoples. In India the Goddess may be shown with hundreds of arms, aptly symbolizing her ability to act for the well being of all creatures at once. Sometimes Hindu gods are depicted with numerous heads or a thousand eyes, indicating their omniscience. For most of history the majority of Indian people—including some of India's greatest saints—have been illiterate. For the sake of conveying complex concepts to functionally illiterate devotees, Hindu artists made frequent use of bizarre-seeming symbolism—like multiple arms—in their images of the divine.

Take for example the image of Lord Ganesha, the delightful, chubby, elephant-headed God who is often painted sitting beside Lakshmi in Indian art, the great being who removes all obstacles and makes the impossible possible, who contains universal knowledge within the vast bulk of his awareness, and who is unfailingly kind. Ganesha has huge, floppy elephant ears because he is attentively listening to the prayers of humanity. He has only one tusk, because he doesn't see the distinction between us and himself; he experiences everything as one vast unity.

While Lord Vishnu rides a giant eagle, Ganesha is shown riding through the world on a mouse! Ganesha is the Higher Self within us, extraordinarily wise, powerful and loving—not unlike an elephant I have to add, in case you've never owned an elephant, as some of my Indian friends have! Like a mighty elephant, the Higher Self can effortlessly remove all obstacles standing between us and our worthy goals, clearing a path through the densest jungle. Our everyday minds are symbolized by the mouse, nibbling at this, nibbling at that, never imagining that we carry inside ourselves the knowledge and strength and extraordinary potential of a much vaster being, the divine Inner Self who "rides" within us. In Hindu mythology, Ganesha guards the door to the Divine Mother's house while she bathes inside. If you wish to see the Goddess unveiled, you must first win the grace of Ganesha, your Higher Self!

If one is in financial difficulties or crushed by misfortune, it is wise to propitiate the Goddess Lakshmi, Hindus believe. You can do this by chanting her mantra, meditating on her, or singing devotional songs to her. Other ways to honor Lakshmi include beautifying yourself and your environment, making charitable donations as generously as she does, or by performing rituals to her in your home or at her temple. It is difficult to attract Lakshmi's grace if one is miserly, slovenly or angry. The Goddess of Wealth is attracted to the home that is loving, harmonious, clean, beautiful, and filled with vibrations of devotion. Happiness begets happiness; Lakshmi prefers to dwell in hearts full of joy and magnanimity. She is extraordinarily generous but expects her devotees to be too. She gives lavishly, though her gifts are not always material. She offers wealth, success, and the fulfillment of sensual desires, but she also bestows spiritual liberation on those rare individuals who ask for it with full sincerity.

Many Indian businesses (especially banks!) and products are named after this Goddess. It is rare to find a Hindu merchant who does not have a painting or statue of Lakshmi in his shop. The Goddess of Prosperity is tremendously popular in South Asia, where she represents overflowing abundance. The problem is that although she is gracious, she is also somewhat skittish, so you must take care to honor her continually so she won't feel ignored, pack her bags and leave.

HONORING LAKSHMI

Of all the major Hindu goddesses, I am most out of tune with Lakshmi. The moment you step into my home you'll notice I didn't decorate it with a possible photo spread in *Homes and Gardens* in mind. The decor in my townhouse is—to put it kindly—functional. No matter how conscientiously I try to style my hair it's always a mess, and no matter how clean my clothes are when I put them on, by the time I get where I'm going there's a smudge on my blouse or a run in my panty hose.

According to Vedic astrology, Venus, the planet representing Lakshmi's energy, is weak in my horoscope. This is the reason I'm not particularly feminine and I'm always broke, according to my Indian astrologer. He's given me a mantra to repeat to propitiate Venus and he recommends that I keep a picture of Lakshmi prominently displayed in my home—this will improve my financial prospects, I'm told.

An officiant at a temple devoted to Raja Rajeshvari (The Supreme Sovereign Empress of the Universe, a particularly spiritually charged form of the Goddess), was also helpful. She taught me a Sanskrit hymn to the Goddess of Wealth which translates:

> With loving reverence I worship Lakshmi,
>> daughter of the king of the ocean of milk,
>> queen of heaven,
>> the seed from which this universe sprouted
>> and the light which illuminates it.
> Due to her sidelong glance
>> the great gods Brahma, Vishnu and Shiva
>> achieved their high positions.
> The Lady of the Lotus is Mother of the Universe,
>> and is the beloved consort of the Supreme Godhead himself.

I was advised to repeat these verses while seated for meditation, visualizing Lakshmi standing in front of me in a red sari embroidered with gold. Her beautiful, pale complexioned face is shining, her dark eyebrows arched coyly. She raises one of her right hands and gently places the palm, reddened with henna, on top of my head. I should be able to feel the warmth and softness of her fingers, my teacher emphasized, and smell the Goddess's lotus fragrance. If a breeze blows into the room during my meditation, I should be able to hear the folds of Lakshmi's sari rustling. Bringing my full attention to the top of my head, I should feel the Goddess's grace pouring into me, warm and golden like liquid honey.

Of course we in the West would say that this type of visualization is merely a way of working with one's subconscious, that unmanageable mass of memories, archetypes and desires which rarely responds to logic. Imagining oneself being blessed by Lakshmi is a clever way to open oneself psychologically to the energies she represents: abundance, good luck, happiness. To Hindus, however, the distinction between inner and outer worlds is not so clear. Yes of course Lakshmi is an energy inside us, yogis would be quick to admit, and could promptly quote dozens of verses from their scriptures to support this claim. But at the same time she is an independent mass of awareness that actually exists in the universe, quite apart from the vivid imaginations of her devotees. There really is a plane of awareness where she dwells, called Devi Loka, "the Goddess World." Even intelligences from other planets can visit her there although they would find that she looks just like them, while we see her as a human female. The Goddess is accommodating and will appear to us in whatever form we're comfortable with.

This unwillingness to dichotomize mental and physical realities is an important distinguishing feature of the tantric tradition. In tantric cosmology, only the tip of our consciousness, conditioned by *ahankara* or the sense of individual selfhood, belongs to us as individuals. The root of our consciousness is submerged in the universal mind. Through the cosmic mind we are linked to all other sentient beings. The Vedic dictum that the sage sees the Self in all beings and all beings in the Self is literally true in this system. As one advances in yoga, mastering the subtler and subtler elements, *siddhis* or psychic powers begin to manifest. What the development of clairvoyance or telepathy really means is that the yogini is coming into deeper awareness of the universal mind. The more she has purified herself of the sense of individual selfhood, the deeper the contact with the cosmic mind will be. The more one's psychic abilities are colored by selfishness, however, the less accurate one's psychic perceptions generally are.

Living in California, I'm continually exposed to would-be psychics whose diagnoses and predictions are wildly inaccurate, steeped in the psychic's desire for fame and fortune. This is a far cry from the saint's ability to heal, protect and inspire. The very first qualification of a seeker aspiring to practice yoga is viveka, the ability to discriminate between what is real and unreal, what is true and untrue. Yoga acknowledges that the greatest force in the universe is *maya,* illusion, and its correlate on the human level is *avidya,* self delusion. *Avidya* laps most psychics up like soft ice cream.

In India spiritual teachers continually warn against cultivating psychic powers for selfish purposes or falling prey to the demon of self-aggrandizement. "True saints do not chase supernatural powers; supernatural powers chase the saints," goes the proverb. Yogis and yoginis who've purified their minds and lovingly worship the Supreme Self in all beings, become conduits through which divine grace spontaneously pours. Miracles happen all around them. In their presence the world becomes an enchanted garden. The saints don't "do" anything—they just get their egos out of the way and allow the Goddess to perform her magic through them.

Too often rather than honoring Lakshmi we want to make her our servant. We want wealth, comfort, prestige, health and good fortune without taking the time to attune ourselves to the divine majesty from which these qualities emanate. We want the fruit but we're too busy indulging ourselves to plant the tree. From Devi Loka, Lakshmi merely smiles.

Within the universal mind, vast intelligences are said to roam. The Goddess Lakshmi is one of them. Because the universal mind is at the base of our own mind, in this sense Lakshmi exists within us. And yet because the cosmic mind is vastly greater than our personal mind, in that sense Lakshmi exists outside ourselves. For the yogini, therefore, the distinction between inner and outer realities is purely artificial. As our awareness grows, the idea that anything exists beyond ourselves gradually dissolves, as does the illusion that we exist anywhere other than in the consciousness of the Supreme One.

Most people pray to Lakshmi for money. The yogini worships Lakshmi for the infinitely vaster wealth of divine knowledge. Lakshmi can remove the barriers between limited and unlimited consciousness with the tiniest stirring of her will. The scriptures claim that those who honor Lakshmi for the totality of what she is eager to give, receive both material largesse and liberating knowledge. Lakshmi wants us to have these things. But in order to acquaint us with our divine nature and our innate spiritual powers, she makes us work for them!

One way we work toward uncovering the divine in ourselves is visualization. When we sit for meditation and picture the Goddess standing outside ourselves or inside our hearts, we are offering her a mental body to manifest through, according to the yogis. If our devotion is truly sincere, it creates a sort of psychic vortex that funnels a fraction of her divine awareness into our meditation. The consciousness/force we call Lakshmi actually exists in a plane utterly beyond words and images, but the dynamic energy of her consciousness can assume a four-armed, crimson-clad form in our mind and bless us or even speak to us. Sometimes the Goddess herself initiates these encounters, appearing to devotees and sometimes even to unsuspecting non-devotees in beautiful and startling visions.

Yogis and yoginis are people too impatient to sit around waiting for the Goddess to appear in her own good time. Focusing their minds intently on her divine attributes or on a picture of her they hold in their imagination, they attempt to consciously draw the Goddess's grace into their lives. The tantras claim that the sincere devotion and one-pointed meditation of spiritual aspirants greatly delights the Goddess. She tests them to ensure their yearning is real, and then graciously enters their lives in the form of a life transforming vision, a spectacular turn of good fortune, a vital spiritual insight, or ineffable bliss.

LAKSHMI TANTRA

Just as we women of the West seek to understand the Goddess today, thousands of years ago in South Asia women sought knowledge of the Feminine Divine. The story of one of these women occurs in the *Lakshmi Tantra,* a Hindu scripture from about the tenth century A.D. It's actually the story of one of the most famous women saints of ancient India, whose name was Anasuya. She was an advanced yogini who attained very high states of consciousness while cooking and cleaning and raising her children. Tales of her intelligence, purity, and strength of character spread so far, they even reached the gods in heaven.

At this point the three greatest gods, Brahma, Vishnu and Shiva, decided to test Anasuya. They entered her home and asked for her hospitality. In the Hindu tradition there is a saying, "The guest is God." In this case it was literally true! Anasuya was of course obligated to fulfill their every request to the best of her ability. The gods asked her to feed them, but it wouldn't be a real test if they didn't make their request as difficult or awkward as possible, so they asked further, "Please take off your clothes and serve us naked." That sounds pretty outrageous to us even today, but in puritanical India it was the most offensive request conceivable.

"As you wish," Anasuya smiled. She waved her hand, turning the gods into infants, opened her sari, and fed the three babies from her breasts. I think this is a wonderful metaphor for how the sanctity of women like Anasuya can transform even the most refractory males.

As the *Lakshmi Tantra* opens, however, Anasuya is mulling over the many philosophies and religious traditions she's studied, and notes a significant omission. She knew little of the secret lore of the Goddess which lay at the root of all tantric training. So she approached her husband Atri, one of the most august sages of his time, and respectfully requested initiation in the great tradition of Lakshmi. She was already familiar with the many external rites commonly practiced to this Goddess, but asked to learn the higher dimensions of the tradition.

"The inner tradition of Lakshmi is deeply sacred and highly esoteric," Atri told her. "I am not allowed to impart this instruction to anyone unless the pupil is truly worthy and asks for the knowledge of his or her own accord. You have always been worthy, my dear one. I am very, very pleased that you have finally come to me seeking knowledge of the Goddess.

"I know you remember how Lakshmi first appeared in her present form. In order to gain everlasting life, the deities and demons were for once cooperating, working together to churn the ocean of milk to produce the nectar of immortality. As they churned, auspicious and inauspicious things emerged from the ocean, poison and ambrosia both. The poison was so dangerous the entire world would have been destroyed if a single drop had spilled. Out of compassion, the great God Shiva sipped the deadly elixir but didn't swallow it. That's why his neck is dark blue—to this day he holds the terrible poison in his throat.

"At last Lakshmi herself, beautiful beyond human imagination and decked with the plenitude of happiness and abundance, stepped out of the sea. As she rose from the water she glanced at the gods but not at the demons. For this reason in the ensuing confrontation over who would drink the nectar, the gods were victorious while the demons perished.

"Of course you understand this is an allegory for inner experiences which occur during meditation. When we coordinate our positive and negative energies, focusing on 'churning' the nerve currents in our spine as we move our awareness up and down through the chakras, we distill the essence of what is best and worst in ourselves. The worst we offer to God. Only he is great enough to contain our inner evil without being affected by it. We must let go of our hatred and selfishness completely and let God carry that burden for us.

"It is through the grace of the Goddess, however, that we taste the nectar of immortality. She offers it to the deities but not the demons. She seeks to nurture only the highest and best in us. She will not feed the demons till they release their rage and self-centeredness. The flavor of immortality is love. The ambrosia would be wasted on the demons until they develop the capacity to love and serve selflessly."

The sage Atri continued the story. Indra, the king of the deities, was celebrating this victory over his enemies. He and his pure hearted allies had quaffed the divine nectar while all around him the demons Spite and Anger and Pettiness lay dying. Brihaspati, the chief priest of the deities, saw that Indra was beginning to swell with pride, so he took him quietly aside. "Remember," he whispered urgently, "you are not the actual victor here. The victory was given to you by the Lady of the Lotus, Lakshmi herself. It is a serious mistake for you to think of yourself as the doer when it fact it is the shakti, the divine energy of the Goddess, which made this great victory possible.

"Surrender yourself, my king, to the Mother of the Universe, the source of the noblest things in life and the final refuge of all creatures. She is the state achieved by the yogi in deepest meditation, the ever-sought goal of spiritual aspirants. All scriptures and all religions and all philosophical systems direct us to her, though they call her by different names. Unless you worship her, what can you possibly achieve? She is the supremely gracious Goddess who satisfies the desires of those given to passion, and leads those devoted to Self-realization toward everlasting beatitude."

Indra instantly recognized the truth in his teacher's words. He immersed himself in prayer and meditation, controlling his senses and focusing his entire awareness on the feet of the Supreme Goddess. Pleased with the intensity of his devotion, Lakshmi assumed a physical form and appeared to the king of the deities. "My darling child, how sincerely you call to me! Your love has touched my heart. I would like to offer you a boon—please tell me what blessing you wish to receive."

Tears of gratitude in his eyes, Indra blurted out, "Divine Mother, please reveal your nature to me. All I want is to know you."

The Tantra says that the Goddess was as delighted with Indra's request as "a milk cow with her calf." With fond affection she began to speak.

"I am Lakshmi, eternal, all pervading, perfect and brimming with beneficence. I am unbounded by space, time or form. I am pure consciousness alone, brimming with ecstacy at the perfection of my own being, the essence of all things.

"I have six divine attributes: (1) perfect knowledge of absolute truth, and (2) perfect sovereignty—the irresistible dynamism of creative will. (3) I am the source of all creation, (4) and my strength is such that with a trillionth part of the potency of my will, I effortlessly create entire universes. (5) Although constant change transpires within me, I myself am unchanging. (6) Everything I desire, I accomplish without external aid. I am completely self-sufficient, abiding ever in my underlying nature of perfect primeval intelligence.

"My purpose in producing the world is to give all beings a

glimpse of their divine nature, revealing the infinite to the finite, and reabsorbing the finite into the infinite. I am the limitless, unchanging majesty of being who creates, controls and annihilates all things. I am also continually evolving in the form of my numberless subjects, whether they are conscious souls or unconscious objects. Everything you behold is me. The very act of seeing is me. And, my cherished child, looking through your eyes, I am the one within you who this very moment is seeing me."

The king of the deities interrupted, "Why then did you create a world in which pleasure coexists with pain? Wouldn't it have been better to make a world in which everyone was happy? If you were going to create so much suffering, why bother to produce a universe at all?"

The Goddess serenely responded, "There is an absolutely pure cosmos within me constituted of knowledge and bliss. Intelligences from this pure creation sometimes enter your plane of existence to give you a glimpse of what your world could be. Ignoring these saints, avatars and divine visitations, you dwell in a mixed cosmos where good and evil, joy and misery, mingle according to your inclination.

"I have given the souls in your universe freedom to choose to act out of love or out of selfish desire. Each soul reaps the fruits of its own thoughts and actions, as well as those of the culture in which it participates. Karma is the instrument I created so that you can understand the consequences of your deeds. It is you who bind yourselves to happiness or suffering. When you experience with the totality of your being that it is I who am the real doer, the deed itself and the object of your action, then you, like me, will become unbounded. You will experience neither good nor evil anywhere, only divine majesty and grace. Then you will devote your life to teaching, serving and protecting others.

"It is just as well for you not to question too hard how or why I do what I do. This vast cosmos is my playground and your lives are my games. I enjoy my own self-existence immensely and I find the coming and going of worlds with all their inhabitants tremendously entertaining. If you relax into your true nature, which is nothing other than my endless bliss, then you will enjoy your sojourn through the material worlds too. Live your life consciously as my playmate. Let us fill the halls of infinity with our laughter. Love all, conscientiously fulfill your responsibilities, do not become overly attached to anyone or anything, and remember in every moment to enjoy yourself. I love you more than you are capable of conceiving. Be joyous!"

Eager to learn more about the Goddess, Indra deluged her with questions about the nature of the universe, the relationship between God and the Goddess, how the Goddess is to be properly worshipped, and mantras with which her divine presence can be invoked. Lakshmi answered patiently, describing specifically how she creates the various types of universes, beginning with the stirring of a billionth of a trillionth part of her will, and ending with the manifestation of the physical elements.

Urged by Indra, Lakshmi also related some of the times she had taken a physical body on Earth. "When there is a special purpose the Supreme Lord Vishnu and I appear together on your planet as human beings, or other times as supernormal beings." For example, she took birth as the princess Sita while her husband Vishnu appeared as the just and compassionate warrior prince Rama. When Vishnu visited the earth in the form of the great teacher called Buddha, Lakshmi again accompanied him, this time in a supernormal form as the Goddess Tara. Sometimes her forms were nonhuman. Once the sages begged her mercy during a long famine and she graced the earth in the guise of Shakambhari, lush and fruitful vegetation.

Lakshmi further explained that Sarasvati, Kali, and the other goddesses are not different from her. There is only one Supreme Goddess, but since she has different functions and appears in a variety of guises in many cultures, devotees give her different names. "Penetrating my disguises and seeing me as I actually am, my devotees are rescued from the unpleasant results of their bad deeds and enter instead my own state of perfect awareness. Those whose minds have been washed clean by the nectar-like flow of meditation on me, experience me as the divine awareness suffusing all creation, including their own hearts.

"How sad that so many beings do not perceive me, even though I reside within them! If someone holds a hibiscus flower up to a clear crystal, the crystal appears red; its true colorless color is not seen. Just so, because like a pure crystal I, the inner awareness, am perfectly transparent, people do not experience me within themselves; rather they focus on their random thoughts and sensations. Those fortunate few on whom I bestow even the minutest fraction of my grace, however, know me as their own continual supreme bliss. One becomes capable of receiving my grace by four means of spiritual practice."

Indra instantly begged Lakshmi to reveal what these four types of practice are.

"The first method is to deliberately free yourself from the cycle of karma. Carry out your rightful responsibilities in the world without polluting your actions by claiming any reward. Renounce the sense that you are performing these activities; remember always that it is my energy and awareness which act through you. At the same time renounce the fruits of your efforts. Act selflessly. Then neither fear nor expectation will bind you. The future will no longer be your concern. You are completely free in the present, an obedient child of the Divine Mother, fulfilling my will in the world.

"The second method is to study experientially the physical and subtle elements ranging from earth, water, fire, air and ether, all the way up to the primeval Self. Learn to distinguish what is material and impermanent from what is everlasting and self-aware. Then open yourself to the divine self-awareness pervading all things.

"The third method is meditation. There are two types of meditation, Indra. The first is to visualize me on the altar before which you are sitting, or on the altar in your heart. Worship me with mantras or other sacred stanzas that bring my divine qualities vividly to your awareness. Offer me gifts like flowers, fragrant scents, delicious foods, beautiful textiles, all the good things your mind can conjure. Then offer yourself. Imagine yourself merging with me in bliss and perfect knowledge. Feel it happen.

"In the second type of meditation you should not visualize anything at all. Divorce yourself from all physical, emotional and mental phenomena. Empty the vessel of your mind completely. Then allow the fullness of my being to pour into you. You will experience peace, happiness and self-knowledge beyond the limits of your imagination.

"When you achieve that state you will enter a realm of absolute splendor, as if millions of sun and moons were shining simultaneously. The great souls who abide in that kingdom remain in full view of the Supreme Lord and myself at all times. They merge in us as he and I merge in each other."

"What is the fourth method you mentioned, Mother?" Indra eagerly inquired.

"One day I was teasing the Lord that these three methods are not as easy as they sound. Mortal beings are bound by the exigencies of time; most pass out of their bodies before they reach the culmination of their spiritual practice. 'Isn't there another way finite souls can realize their infinite nature?' I asked my husband. 'A quicker, surer way?'

"Vishnu laughed and answered, 'My dearest Self, you know the answer as well as I. Out of compassion for suffering beings, you have asked me to elaborate what you already know. Total surrender to me is the easiest and best way to achieve perfect enlightenment.'"

"Wait, wait!" Indra interrupted. "Total surrender—what does that actually mean?"

"It means one should respect all beings throughout the universe as much as one respects God himself, recognizing the thorough divinity of the entire cosmos and all the creatures within it. Give up all arrogance, acting instead for the benefit of all living things in a spirit of deep humility. Know that I am everywhere, in everything, and act accordingly.

"When you adopt this sacred way of thinking, feeling and behaving, fragrant petals of faith will blossom in your heart. You will be purified very rapidly and quite soon you will begin to actually experience the divine in every aspect of life. Everywhere you step, you will feel my loving embrace. My all enveloping compassion will become your nature. Taking refuge in me means taking refuge in your unity with all creation. You will discover that you are unlimited. Then your love also will be limitless.

"When the ocean floods the shore, you can't see dry land anywhere. Just so, my divine essence floods the universe. There is no particle anywhere devoid of my presence. Just as bees gather pollen in order to create honey, so yogis and yoginis gather experiences of me in order to taste bliss. Everything their minds dwell on they perceive to be me. They see the elements as flowers strung together on

a garland hanging around my neck. The world is a beautiful painting to them, and I am the canvas."

Indra's mind was reeling with ecstacy. "Mother, I cannot find
words sufficient to praise or thank you," he stammered.

"Remember, my son, that when I first manifested myself in
perceptible form, I deliberately chose to appear in a female body,"
Lakshmi smiled. "Therefore a person devoted to spiritual practice
should never, ever abuse a woman, not physically, not verbally, not
even in thought. I am inherent in all women and in the material
universe itself. Therefore anyone who disdains women disdains me,
while anyone who honors women simultaneously loves and praises
the entire cosmos. The devotee who loves and respects women,
never thinking an evil thought about them, is very close to me.
Since women are my direct embodiments, yogis should revere and
worship them, never even imagining that evil can exist in them.
Men who wish to become enlightened should show the highest
respect toward women, regarding every woman they meet as their
mother and as my human emanation.

"When a male devotee makes love to a woman, he should free
his mind from lust, contemplating her beauty as my own and her
soul as my own Self. For him, sexual union should be a glorious
meditation on the Goddess. The pleasure he experiences is my
pleasure; let him recognize this. Similarly, a woman should envision
her lover as the Lord himself, perfect and blissful. Enjoyment based
solely on lust has a beginning and an end. Enjoyment based on the
conscious acknowledgment of my all pervading perfection is
endless.

"Surrender to me totally. Then I will totally surrender everything
I am to you."

Atri concluded his exposition of the *Lakshmi Tantra* by
reciting the lineage of men and women sages who had passed
along the hidden knowledge of the Goddess Lakshmi for untold
generations. "My dear wife," he finished, "please ponder this Tantra
with a heart free from prejudice and rancor. Focus your mind continually on Vishnu and Lakshmi, the Supreme Godhead and the
Supreme Goddess, understanding their unity. Do not torment yourself with guilt or grief if in some thoughtless moment you commit
a sin—if you sincerely cherish the divine couple, they have already

freed you from the consequences of your error. Maintaining an attitude of honest humility, devote yourself to helping others.

"Anasuya, these teachings I have imparted are highly sacred. You are now qualified to instruct other sincere aspirants, but you must never share these teachings with people who are hostile or cynical, with those who disparage marriage, or with anyone who disrespects women."

Anasuya bowed before her saintly husband, then went to sit before the image of the Goddess in her shrine room. Merging her awareness in divine being, Anasuya experienced complete sublimity. Then she rose and, bearing the living Goddess in her heart, resumed the joyful and sacred task of serving her family.

GOD AND GODDESS

Many of the Hindu goddesses, though linked with male consorts, for the most part act on their own. Lakshmi however, as protectress and sanctioner of married life, is always associated with her husband Vishnu. The classic *Vishnu Purana* describes the divine couple in these terms:

> Vishnu is knowledge; Lakshmi is understanding.
> Vishnu is righteousness; Lakshmi is righteous action.
> Vishnu is the sun; Lakshmi is the sunlight.
> Vishnu is the moon; Lakshmi is the moon's glowing radiance.
> Vishnu is space; Lakshmi is the sky.
> Vishnu is the ocean; Lakshmi is the shore.
> Vishnu holds the weapon; Lakshmi is might.
> Vishnu is the groom; Lakshmi is the bride.
> Vishnu is love; Lakshmi is passion.
> Vishnu is all pervading; Lakshmi also pervades all things.
> Vishnu and Lakshmi are all existence;
> there is nothing beyond these two-in-one.

The Hindu scriptures are rife with passages which portray God as being and the Goddess as becoming. Brahma is the Creator God, but Sarasvati is the power which creates. Vishnu upholds the universe but Lakshmi enacts the divine will. At the end of the eon, Shiva wipes the universe out of existence but his wife Parvati is the limitless power through which this occurs. Let stanzas like these put an end to the absurd but widely accepted myth that all human societies consider the male principle active and the female principle passive! For thousands of years, the Hindu tantric tradition has taught exactly the opposite.

Although the Hindu Goddess tradition acknowledges the sentiment that God or Vishnu is Self and the Goddess or Lakshmi is Self-awareness, it specifically clarifies that the concepts of Vishnu/Lakshmi or Shiva/Shakti are ultimately nothing more than verbal nuances, different ways of describing an identical, nondual reality. Westerners sometimes have a difficult time grasping this type of blithe philosophic reconciliation. We have grown up in a culture which sees things in terms of black and white, which requires students to answer test questions with "True" or "False," and witnesses in the courtroom to respond with "Yes" or "No." True/False exams are virtually unknown in India; almost all tests require essay answers, reflecting the Asian view that few matters in life are so straightforward they can be answered with a simple yes or no. When I first started studying Hindu philosophy I was surprised by how much at ease my Indian professors were with apparently opposing points of view. They were as much at home with the system which claims the universe is composed of material atoms (this system, called Vaisesika, was current in India centuries before Leucippus and Democritus began teaching a similar doctrine in Greece) as with the system which claims the universe is composed of consciousness alone. All systems propounded by enlightened sages were accepted as equally valid, even when they appeared to completely contradict each other!

Well, it doesn't take long living in the right brained culture of India for questions like these to dissolve. Paradoxes such as "God is completely transcendent and doesn't act in the world" versus "God creates, sustains and reabsorbs the world" exist only in words; the indescribable reality these conflicting statements point toward is coherent and sublime. In Hinduism, God and Goddess can be both separate entities and one single being, divine consciousness and matter can be both radically differentiated and perfectly unified. The distinction exists only in limited awareness; when consciousness becomes unlimited, distinctions disappear.

A physiologist giving you an examination will note how your bones, muscles, and nerve fibers work together. A physicist analyzing you will see something very different: the play of subatomic forces interacting across fields of empty space. A chemist will note instead the interplay of myriad molecular compounds within your cells. A geneticist observes self-replicating DNA at work. A psychologist, however, notes a personality in the throes of various complexes. All these ways of describing you are completely accurate, even though they employ such different terminology that scientists in these different fields can barely understand each other and, viewed superficially, their descriptions seem to have little in common.

The same thing happened when the yogis and philosophers of India turned their attention to the Goddess. Some saw her as *prakriti*, the material substrate of the universe. Others saw her as *maya*, the force which limits and conditions our ability to perceive the total interconnectedness of all things. Still others described her as *shakti*, primeval cosmic energy that is self-willed and self-aware. Some experienced her simply as *mata*, mother. None of these views is even remotely adequate to describe her. All of them are nevertheless accurate.

Many cultures have anthropomorphized the divine, projecting the dualities we experience in life (right and wrong, active or passive, transcendent and imminent) onto an underlying reality which defies all categorizations. Most cultures also split divine being into masculine and feminine components, and a few go so far as to eliminate the feminine aspect altogether. It is inconceivable to the Hindu to imagine God without the Goddess, as Christians, Jews and Muslims do.

A few years ago here in Northern California, a group of Westerners who had embraced Hinduism enthusiastically built a temple to their favorite God, Lord Shiva. They were shocked when Indian Hindus refused to worship there. It turned out the Indians considered a temple in which the Goddess was ignored extremely inauspicious! Shiva would never feel comfortable in a temple in which his wife was slighted. The Western devotees quickly installed a statue of Shiva's wife Parvati, and Indians gladly began attending services.

In India it is perfectly legitimate—and to some it's actually preferable—to speak of the divine as genderless transcendent being, but those who do so generally use a neuter term like *parabrahman* (the all expansive) or *samvit* (the self-existent). Goddess worshipers sometimes deliberately refer to genderless Supreme Being with feminine names like Tripura Sundari or Sri Vidya. This is a purposeful metaphor designed to steer the mind away from thinking of "the Absolute" as a great void or as completely impersonal. It's hard to love a void! Deliberately reformulating one's mental picture of "the self-existent," transforming it into, for example, Maha Lakshmi (Cosmic Lakshmi), helps spiritual aspirants to marshall not only their intellects but also their deepest feelings into a veritable love affair with the divine. They enter into a relationship with the transcendent and often experience divine imminence much more quickly than those yogis dutifully regulating their breath while chanting mantras to a formless void.

Obviously, not every Hindu is interested in experiencing divinity. Many, perhaps most, would prefer to experience the delightful clink of hard, cold coins. Lakshmi understands this and lovingly grants the requests of her sincere worshipers for health and longevity, good looks, a faithful spouse, children, fertile fields ripe with bountiful crops, and successful businesses. It is also her grace which maintains social order. When she withdraws her favor, rulers lose power. As the ancient *Rig Veda* counsels, "Honor wealth. Earn it through hard work performed ethically, and through worship." Lakshmi, the Goddess of Wealth, is one Indian deity who never lacks for worshipers.

During Divali, the Hindu Festival of Lights, Lakshmi is especially feted. On this holiday Hindu farmers ritually honor their harvest and shopkeepers their account books. Thus they symbolically attune themselves to the cosmic force which provides for their basic needs and—sometimes—fulfills their desire for luxuries.

In Hindu art, when Lakshmi is shown with her consort, she and Vishnu are always portrayed as a loving, sensual couple. In one common pose, God is reclining in bed while the Goddess massages his feet, the two gazing rapturously into each other's eyes. This scene might seem to reflect India's patriarchal order, the submissive wife sitting adoringly at her lord's feet, but the symbolism is actually more complex. When it comes to the Goddess who governs *maya,* appearances are often deceiving.

The Glory of the Goddess

Devi Mahatmyam (The Glory of the Goddess) opens with the tale of two lost souls, the deposed king Suratha and the ruined merchant Samadhi. Both had been enormously successful men, but Suratha was betrayed by his ministers and Samadhi's hard earned fortune was stolen by greedy relatives. They encountered each other in a forest, where both were wandering homeless and destitute. After commiserating about their unhappy fates, they decided to approach the sage Medhas for spiritual counseling.

"Why is it," they asked, "that after having personally experienced the fleeting nature of power and wealth, we still crave these things? Why is it that although our friends and relations have betrayed us, we still love them and long to be reunited with them?"

"Ah yes," Medhas sighed, "we all seem to be deluded, don't we, prey to our own desires. Every living thing acts out of greed and selfishness, perceiving only as much of the infinite totality as its pitifully limited senses allow it to see. This dream of a world and our compulsive desires for its dream pleasures are the work of the Goddess Maha Maya, the force of cosmic illusion. She seizes even the minds of the wise and drags them to their destruction. It was she who created this threefold universe in the first place, then catches us in the web of its illusions. But it is also she who can free us from this bondage because she is the Supreme Empress of the worlds. The chimeras she created she can just as easily destroy."

"Tell us more about this Goddess," the king and the merchant pleaded.

"She is without beginning or end but she appears in the form of this world which came into existence some billions of years ago and will pass out of existence some billions of years hence," the sage replied. "Though she herself was never born, she takes birth in response to the prayers of her devotees.

"Many billions of years ago the universe before ours passed out of existence. No longer having the affairs of limitless creatures to attend to or any more crises to resolve, God took a nap. He stretched out on his couch and as the Goddess Lakshmi gently massaged his divine feet he passed into the state of *yoga nidra,* yogic sleep. Now while Vishnu was resting, the Creator God Brahma was stirring, drawing up plans for the next universe. But then suddenly he was attacked by two powerful demons who somehow had managed to escape from Vishnu's dream. Brahma raced over to Vishnu to beg for protection but the Supreme Lord was sound asleep, and no matter how urgently he tugged on his sleeve, Brahma could not get Vishnu to wake up. He realized he needed the help of Vishnu's wife and fervently invoked her:

"'You are the Supreme Mother, the primeval vibration out of which the universe manifests in wave after wave of divine energy. You lovingly protect the creatures born from your radiant divine womb, and when the cycle of time has run its course you absorb all creatures back into the tomb of your timeless being.

"'You are Maha Maya, the great illusion of time and space and cause and effect. You are also Maha Vidya, the great knowledge which lifts us beyond space and time and causality. You are insight into the nature of things, and memory of our real, timeless essence. Yes, you are the Great Goddess but you are the Great Demonness also. You impale souls on the spear of matter where they experience you as the great night of destruction, the terrible night of suffering and disease and death and delusion.

"'And yet you are Lakshmi, full of beauty and auspiciousness. Souls experience you as modesty, intelligence, contentment, tranquility and forgiveness. At the same time you are the invincible warrioress whose weapons are indomitable. Yet you are most gentle, most beautiful, the greatest of all, the Supreme Empress.

"'Everything, anything, whether it exists or not, abides in you. You are the infinite shakti, the unfathomable power that gives existence to existence. How, then, is it possible to find words adequate to praise you?

"'And yet look at what you've done! Overcome by your power, my benefactor Lord Vishnu lies here unconscious. How ever can I describe your power which overwhelms even God himself? You created Vishnu, Shiva, and myself yet you lie utterly beyond our petty fiefdoms of creation, protection and destruction. You are unfathomable—even God can't begin to understand your power!

"'Please, Mother, throw your spell of confusion over the demons who want to destroy me and allow my protector Vishnu to wake up! I desperately need his help!'

"Pleased by Brahma's devotion, the Goddess withdrew her veil of nescience from the Supreme God, and Vishnu opened his eyes. Seeing his friend Brahma under attack, he grabbed his weapons and ran out to slay the two would-be assassins. They were remarkably tenacious demons though, known as Me and Mine, and he couldn't seem to make any headway against them.

"At last the Goddess intervened, casting her spell of *maya* over the devils. Puffed up with the sense of their mightiness—this was God they were holding at bay here—they sneered at Vishnu, "Hey you weak one, ask for a boon. Let us show you the full extent of our power!"

"'I have only one request,' Vishnu panted, 'that you allow yourselves to be killed by me.'

"The demons glanced at each other and swallowed hard. Then looking around they noticed that, the material universe having vanished, nothing was left in existence but the primeval waters. This vast ocean—the substrate of matter/energy from which atoms are created—extended forever. 'Okay,' they leered. 'But there's one condition. You can't kill us on any ground covered with water.'

"Vishnu grinned, placed them both on his dry lap, and sliced off their heads.

"And so you see," Medhas concluded, "how the Goddess is both suffering and safe haven. Even God acts or fails to act at her command. If she can delude the Lord himself, no wonder we're so confused!"

The medieval theologian Mamunikal writes, "Lakshmi enslaves the Lord with her beauty, glancing coyly at him from the corner of her eyes and allowing her sari to slip provocatively." She does the same thing to us, blessing and cursing us with desire for sex, a comfortable life, fame or notoriety, and ecstatic meditative states. When the fullness of Lakshmi's grace begins to flow, however, true devotees are able to walk a fine line, appreciating the gifts Lakshmi bestows but not allowing themselves to become enslaved by them. As the late tantric master Aghoreshvara Bhagavan Ramaji used to say, "Be like the ant which sips the sugar syrup while walking carefully around it, not like the greedy fly which dives into the sweet syrup and drowns." Such illumined devotees are Lakshmi's greatest delight.

We will return to the adventures of Suratha and the merchant Samadhi in the next chapter. In the meantime, I will close with a favorite hymn chanted by millions of Hindus daily to invoke Lakshmi's blessings of prosperity at all levels. May the Great Goddess release us from the grip of feverish delusion and grant us the lasting vision of her blissful being, as well as health, happiness, abundance and success!

Maha Lakshmi Stotram:

In Praise of Abundant Joy

With loving reverence I bow to the Supreme Goddess
    Lakshmi, you who cause the universe to appear!
You are the overflowing abode of abundance
    and are joyously worshiped by all the gods!
You are armed with the conch and the mace.
I bow again with gratitude and awe.

With loving reverence I bow to the Supreme Goddess
    Lakshmi, you who sit astride the great eagle of divine
    protection!
You terrify the demons around us and within us
    and graciously nullify their power!
You are the loving one loved by all.
I bow again with gratitude and awe.

All knowing, ever generous,
    gracious destroyer of evil,
    you are the beloved remover of sorrow!
I bow again with gratitude and awe.
With great delight, you grant intelligence and success,
    pleasure and spiritual perfection.
You are the essence and the potency of the sacred mantra!
I bow again with gratitude and awe.

You are the eternal, limitless, luminous,
    primeval cosmic energy, the Supreme Goddess!
You are directly experienced in deep meditation.
I bow again with gratitude and awe.

The subtle and material worlds exist in you,
    created and destroyed by your unfathomable power!
Beloved Goddess, you instantly forgive even the most
    abhorrent sins.
I bow again with gratitude and awe.

Seated on a lotus, you are the embodiment
    of the Supreme Reality.
Great Goddess, you are the devoted Mother of All!
I bow again with gratitude and awe.

Clothed in light, glittering like priceless gems,
    you, the grace-filled World Mother,
    uphold the entire universe!
I bow again with gratitude and awe.

Whosoever recites this praise even once
    with deep reverence and devotion,
    attains success and rulership,
    granted by Lakshmi's abounding grace.

Whoever recites this praise once each day
    is freed from guilt and fear.
Whoever recites this praise twice each day
    lives in perpetual abundance.

Whoever recites this praise three times each day
    gains complete self mastery.
The Supreme Goddess Lakshmi loves this victor
    and pours out her blessings unceasingly!

4

Durga
The Goddess as Conquering Power

Rama was in tears. During the last few years he had lost nearly everything, including the kingdom he'd been destined to rule and his late, beloved father. Through years of wandering in exile, he had maintained his equanimity and sense of humor, sustained by the philosophy of life an old priest named Vasishtha had taught him when he was a child. But this final loss broke him completely.

Rama had returned to his forest campsite and found that his wife Sita had vanished into thin air. Hour after hour, week after week, he frantically searched for her, hardly daring to hope she was still alive. Now at last there was news: it turned out Sita had been abducted by Ravanna, the king of Sri Lanka, and was being held captive in his citadel. Rama thought of his gentle, beautiful wife at the mercy of a monster like Ravanna and tears burst from his eyes.

Ravanna was the most powerful king in South Asia; his wealthy kingdom lay across a wide channel. Rama, after years of struggling for survival in the jungle, had no boat, no army, no money, no allies, and no hope. How could he possibly help Sita? Weeping in the forest, Rama seriously contemplated ending his life.

There was a rustle in the branches above as the sage Narada alighted from the sky, cheerfully humming a hymn from the *Vedas*. Rama leapt up and offered the saint the only thing he had to give, a handful of clean water for washing the seer's feet.

"Oh my, my, Rama, how upset you are, sitting here moping like a child!" Narada scolded. "You, of all men, should know better! I just wanted to let you know I've seen Sita, reflected in the mirror of the cosmic mind. She's being kept closely guarded in Ravanna's garden, and she's quite safe. She thinks of you every moment. It's your destiny to kill Ravanna and destroy his wicked empire for once and for all, you know."

Rama stared at the sage in astonishment. "Sri Lanka is the most heavily fortified kingdom in the world. How can I possibly conquer Ravanna?"

"Surely you know the answer to that! Remember what Jupiter did when the Moon stole his wife. Jupiter got Tara back, didn't he? Remember what Indra and the other demi-gods always do when they're in serious trouble, and what illustrious seers like Bhrigu and Vishvamitra and Kashyapa do when things go sour. Fast for nine days and nights, perform the fire ritual according to the ancient rites, chant the sacred mantras, and invoke the Mother of the Universe. Worship the Divine Mother with your whole heart, and she will remove every difficulty. The three greatest of the gods, Brahma, Vishnu and Shiva, the forces of creation, protection and destruction themselves, run to the Supreme Goddess whenever there's a crisis so big even they can't handle it."

"Please wait," Rama cried. "Who is this Goddess? What is her name? Where can I find her? Tell me everything about her!"

"She is the eternal creative energy of the universe," Narada replied. "Those who worship her with sincere reverence find that all their desires are fulfilled. She is the source from which the great gods arose at the beginning of time. All living beings are rooted in her. She is life energy itself; without her, you couldn't even lift your little finger. While all sentient beings, all gods, all galaxies, are born from her, she herself was never born and will never pass away. She is the living, breathing, self-existent reality itself.

"It's the Mother of the Universe who empowers the gods to fulfill their functions. She is the source of both matter and energy. She is spiritual knowledge and liberating power. Different beings in different worlds have different names for her. It's impossible for me to even begin to list them all! Worship the Goddess who is power itself and she'll give you conquering power."

With Narada's assistance, Rama performed the Nava Ratri Puja (the ritual lasting nine nights), worshiping the Divine Mother, his heart brimming with devotion and faith. As he finished the rite, an immense form took shape in the clearing in front of him. It was a woman seated on a lion, each of her many hands wielding a deadly weapon. The Goddess Durga's voice resonated like the rumbling of a thundercloud. "I am satisfied with your worship," she announced. "Your desire will be fulfilled. You will vanquish Ravanna and find your Sita.

"But Rama, in order to conquer Ravanna, you must understand your true identity. My boon to you is self-knowledge. Rama, God is alive within you. You have incarnated yourself many times to save the helpless. This time you took birth in response to the prayers of the suffering and oppressed who have been calling out for rescue from the evil king Ravanna.

"At this very moment, I am sending powerful allies to aid your cause. You will destroy Ravanna and regain your lost kingdom where you will reign justly and mercifully for many years. Finally you will return to your true abode in a higher state of consciousness. Commemorate your victory over Ravanna every autumn by worshiping me with this same nine-night-long ritual. Receive my blessing, fight for justice, and trust in the upcoming victory I have already granted you."

This is one of many stories which appear in the *Devi Bhagavatam,* a Hindu classic celebrating the interventions of the Goddess in Earth's affairs. And as every Hindu child knows, Rama was soon joined by an army of intelligent, devoted animals—monkeys and bears and even chipmunks—who helped him build a land-bridge between the Indian subcontinent and Sri Lanka. His ragtag army was then able to cross into Sri Lanka and, against seemingly insurmountable odds, brought the bloody reign of Ravanna to an end. In an epiphany of joy, Rama and Sita were finally reunited.

And that is why to this very day, each autumn Hindus in every corner of the globe celebrate Nava Ratri (the nine nights), a major Hindu religious festival, honoring the goddesses Sarasvati, Lakshmi, and especially Durga, the Goddess who unfailingly grants victory to those who cherish her.

It certainly would be nice if the Goddess really did materialize in front of our eyes in response to our prayers. And incredibly, *she does.* Visitations from the Divine Mother are common in India.

When Mother Teresa died in September 1997, I watched in stunned disbelief as Western journalists depicted India as a country where Hindus leave the poor to die in the streets, and deliberately made it appear as if Mother Teresa singlehandedly walked the streets of Calcutta to rescue the sick and dying. Having lived in Calcutta, I've personally witnessed the herculean efforts of the Indian people to help their own poor, but the Hindu doctors who work night and day without pay to aid the suffering, the Hindu housewives who distribute food to the starving, the government officials struggling to help with the limited resources their country can afford—none of these heroes was ever mentioned in the news reports. Nor did Western reporters explain that it is the non-stop flood of refugees from Muslim Bangladesh who ensure that Calcutta's streets are perpetually lined with beggars. These penniless immigrants who daily pour over the border into Calcutta simply overwhelm the city's ability to absorb and find work for them. India is a land filled with living saints, many of whom work tirelessly for the poor, but for the last few decades only one saint in India ever found her way into the Western press: a white-skinned, European-born Catholic nun. When it comes to attention from Western news services, dark-skinned, native born Hindus need not apply. How ironic that a great soul like Mother Teresa, a woman who deeply loved India, should become an unwitting icon for white racism!

In the same way, the Divine Mother's appearances at Guadalupe, Fatima, Lourdes, and lately at Medjugorje have been widely reported in the West, yet most Americans and Europeans have no idea that she has also been manifesting in India and China. Perhaps this is because when she appears in China she takes the form of Quan Yin, a form the Chinese instantly recognize, while in India she appears as Sarasvati or Lakshmi or Durga. In each country she graciously assumes whatever form the people of that culture understand her through, using that guise to pull us back into her lap. At sites like Medjugorje she uses Christian terminology to encourage us to reform ourselves and turn back to the divine. In India she may speak Hindi or Tamil, but her message is the same: "Love each other. Remember that there is a greater reality behind the material realm. Don't be afraid. I am here."

Here on the outskirts of a tiny village not far from the Bay of Bengal, I am sitting on the very spot where the Mother of the

Universe appeared to Baba Dulal not many years ago. She towered over him in the lonely forest setting where he had been doing intensive meditation, her head brushing the top branches of the trees. She appeared in the form of Durga, the Warrior Goddess—the form of the Goddess Rama worshiped thousands of years ago.

I know exactly what Baba Dulal saw because shortly before his death, he commissioned an artist to create a life size *murti* of his vision. Towering twenty feet in the air, the statue of Durga is so powerfully alive, my breath stops each time I look up at it. But even more vivid than the *murti* is the Goddess's fragrance, which still lingers in the atmosphere of the sanctuary built to commemorate the visitation. Her perfume is the unworldly sense of peace which, years after her visit, still hangs in the air. The evidence for the reality of the Goddess's manifestation here is that for hundreds of yards in every direction from the spot where she materialized, one's mind simply and effortlessly glides into a state of absolute serenity. This is one of the most magical sites I've experienced in my life. It's just unbelievable. Merely by coming near this sacred site, pilgrims are thrust into higher levels of consciousness.

Durga's face, carefully recreated by Baba Dulal's artist, is extra-ordinary. Though the *murti* is laden with swords and scimitars, bows and batons, her features are serene. Durga doesn't attack because she's angry. She attacks because we've invited her to liber-ate us from our inner demons. Durga is our Mother and her victory is our victory, even though it hurts like hell. Ravanna—the selfish-ness and egotism, greed and hatred within us—has to be destroyed so that Sita, our innermost soul, can be reunited with God. Amazingly, the instant Rama killed Ravanna, Ravanna was liberated and flew straight to the highest heaven! That's because when the evil in us is vanquished by the divine force, it's not annihilated or suppressed but transformed, its energy released and redirected to act for everyone's benefit rather than for our self undoing.

As the expression on the face of the demon writhing at Durga's feet vividly illustrates, this process of purification is genuinely painful, at least as long as we continue to cling to our desires and attachments, refusing to surrender them to the universal process which will rip them away from us at death anyway. The challenge is to reflect the same compassion and tranquility radiating from

Durga's face in our own hearts, even as we feel her swords and batons, in the form of disease, disappointment, accidents, old age and death, battering our lives.

The *Chandi*

King Suratha and the merchant Samadhi were struggling to meet this challenge as they sat at the feet of the sage Medhas, learning about Goddess Durga. The scripture describing this episode, as I mentioned in the last chapter, is called the *Devi Mahatmyam,* but the village people know it as the *Chandi,* and it's one of the most sacred and frequently chanted texts in all of India. My husband and I have sat through the chanting of the *Chandi* many times, throwing our offerings of rice and barley grains into the ritual fire each time the priest pauses to shout, "Svaha!" "Please accept our sacrifice!"

I've already related the first episode of the *Chandi,* in which the Goddess releases Vishnu the Protector from his yogic slumber in order to rescue Brahma the Creator. The Goddess doesn't require a male deity to do her fighting for her, however. Here is the rest of the story, as Medhas related it to the king and the merchant.

The demon Mahisha defeated the demi-gods after a bitter hundred-year war, and threw the virtuous deities out of heaven. Stealing their powers and treasures, he terrorized the three worlds: the physical world, the mental world, and the still more subtle spiritual world beyond the mental plane. Meanwhile the demi-gods rushed to the court of the great gods Brahma, Vishnu and Shiva to plead for help.

When the great gods learned about the terrible injustices Mahisha was perpetrating in the lower worlds, they became furious. Laser-like rays blazed from their foreheads and merged into a united mass of fiery light, huge and volatile and terrifying as an erupting volcano. One by one each of the demi-gods standing nearby focused his mind and added the full force of his concentration to the flaming effulgence.

Gradually the blinding light assumed the form of a woman. Her heart-breakingly beautiful face emerged from the light projected by Lord Shiva, her breasts from the light radiating from Lord Chandra, the Moon. Her two eyebrows were formed by the lords of Dawn and Dusk, and the tips of her toes shone with the splendor of Lord Surya, the Sun. Each of the deities gave her the subtle essence of his own weapon. Shiva gave her his trident, Vishnu his deadly whirling discus. Yama, the lord of death, gave her the bludgeon with which he strikes his victims at their appointed hour. Vishvakarma, the cosmic architect, gave her a suit of impenetrable armor, and Indra, the king of the demi-gods, gave her his flaring thunderbolt. The Milky Way offered her beautiful ornaments, earrings and bracelets and anklets and a brilliant crest-jewel of stars. Kubera, the lord of treasure, gave her an exquisite goblet perpetually brimming with intoxicating wine, and the Himalayas presented her with the largest, fiercest lion from its mountain domain so she could ride it triumphantly into battle.

There is a fundamental tantric principle being illustrated in this portion of the *Chandi*. Hindus believe the Goddess incarnates in the lower three worlds in response to the prayers of her devotees. Sometimes she is born in a human body, as for example when she took birth as the extraordinary sage Anandamayi Ma in East Bengal in 1896, or as the great humanitarian Ammachi, born near Cochin in 1953. Both women, Hindus say, were born fully enlightened, having emerged directly from the limitless consciousness of the Supreme. More often the Goddess simply temporarily borrows a body, a phenomenon frequently reported in village India even today, when the Goddess or one of her emanations "possesses" a woman, helping to solve critical problems of even her poorest, illiterate devotees. Sometimes she appears as an apparition, manifesting in semi-material form before a group of devotees (Westerners have also seen this happen, for example, at Medjugorje), and other times she enters the minds of those who worship her in a vision or a lucid dream to provide guidance, comfort and healing.

The Goddess incarnates in both female and male forms. For example, five thousand years ago when much of North India was overrun by aggressive warriors, Bhu Devi (the Earth Goddess better known in the West today by her Greek name Gaia) prayed for freedom from this burden of violent, malicious human males. According to the *Devi Bhagavatam,* the Supreme Goddess obligingly took birth on earth in the form of Lord Krishna, the prince of Mathura who orchestrated the true first World War, embroiling troops from as far away as southern Europe and Indonesia in a huge conflict in which hundreds of thousands of soldiers and mercenaries were killed. This epochal battle is described in India's great epic, the *Mahabharata*. It's a vivid example of how an event which seems like an unparalleled disaster to humanity may actually be the Goddess's blessing to another life form seeking her help.

Krishna is the male *avatar* most loved by women in India because of his special attunement to women and to feminine needs. For example, once an army raided a kingdom near Krishna's own, killing many inhabitants and taking thousands of women captive. The local men were afraid to pursue the marauders because they were so powerful and dangerous, but as soon as he heard that the lives of women were at stake, Krishna fearlessly led a small band to free them. Ironically, rescuing the women left them in an even worse position than they'd been in in the camps of their attackers. According to the laws of their area, women who had been raped were "impure" and could not be accepted back by their families. ("Blaming the victim," sadly, goes back a long way!)

When the women tearfully explained why they could never go home, Krishna was enraged. Summoning a priest, in perhaps the most remarkable mass wedding in history, Krishna married every woman there on the spot! He then sent each woman home with explicit instructions to her father that if she wasn't welcomed home as the bride of the prince of Mathura, her father would have to answer to Krishna personally! It's no wonder many Shaktas in India even today believe Krishna was a male incarnation of the Goddess.

But there is still another way in which the Goddess can enter our lives. In the tantric tradition, yogis and yoginis often visualize the Goddess in painstaking detail, lovingly worshiping the form they've given her in their minds. In this case rather than offering her a physical body to manifest through, the devotees are building a non-physical body shaped from mental matter in which she can incarnate. Their intense devotion creates a vortex through which the grace of the Goddess pours, infusing the image they hold of her in their minds, which then comes to life to guard, advise and enlighten them.

In the *Chandi* the gods are not creating a Goddess out of the light of their own imaginations. They are instead consciously constructing a body through which the unborn, undying Mother of the Universe can manifest in their plane of reality.

Having assumed the shape of the invincible warrioress Durga, the Supreme Goddess roared with laughter so terrifyingly loud that its echoes shook the worlds. Feeling the ground shaking and seeing the mountains erupting with flaming lava, the evil usurper Mahisha quickly summoned his army. In the distance the demons saw the cause of the commotion, a woman so stupendously huge her head grazed the sky while the ground sank beneath the weight of her feet. Twanging a gigantic bow string with her thousand arms, she invited the demons to battle.

Massing by the thousands, Mahisha's troops attacked. Playfully and without any sign of fatigue, the Mother of the Universe launched one volley of arrows after another. Every one of Durga's exhalations was a mantra, and from each mantra sprang millions of more demi-goddesses, heavily armed and bloodthirsty. The battle drums beaten by the goddesses sounded so powerfully that even after the demon's heads had been struck off, their decapitated bodies vibrated to the pounding beat as though they were dancing. The demons were so terrified that as their severed heads rolled across the ground, their mouths still shouted, "Stop! Please stop!" In only a few moments the goddesses had swept through Mahisha's troops like a forest fire through dry grass. Durga stood laughing as her lion prowled the battlefield, searching for any breathing body among the dead to maul.

But Mahisha wasn't finished. He had been holding his mightiest commanders in reserve. Now the demon chiefs rushed toward the Goddess. One by one Durga picked them off with her javelin, arrows, trident, spear and mace. In the end, only Mahisha himself was left standing.

Assuming the form of a massive buffalo, Mahisha shook the landscape with the pounding of his hooves and ripped mountains out of the earth with his horns. His flailing tail slapping the ocean caused the coasts to flood. Durga lassoed him with her noose but he slipped out easily, shapeshifting into the form of a lion. As Durga's axe came down on his head he metamorphosed into a human soldier; as her sword was about to strike this armored knight, he transformed into an elephant. As the Goddess struck, he changed yet again, back into his buffalo form.

The Mother of the Universe roared with laughter and took a deep draught of wine, her eyes reddening with intoxication. Mahisha the buffalo, intoxicated with himself, bellowed his invincibility. At that moment Durga leapt onto the buffalo, pinning his throat with her foot and driving her trident into his heart. The demon king tried to escape through the buffalo's gaping mouth but it was too late. Before he could drag himself from the stiffening corpse, Durga caught him by the hair and slit his throat. The entire universe reverberated with the victory shouts of the delighted demi-gods, as they made their way back to their rightful places in heaven.

Everywhere I traveled in India, Durga's conquest of Mahisha was depicted. It's sculpted in temples, but pictures of the victory scene appear also at produce stands and in sari shops. At the home of a wealthy devotee I visited in Calcutta, a stunningly beautiful painting of Durga, glowing with divine luster, her trident piercing the buffalo demon's hide, held pride of place on the living room wall.

Western students may be excused if it's difficult for them to grasp what all the fuss is about. To non-Hindus unable to understand the beautiful Sanskrit verses, resonant with sacred mantras, the story told in the *Chandi* sounds violent and bizarre. A valuable clue in learning to appreciate the *Chandi* is that it is an immense favorite of the yogis. It is to the yogic tradition we need to turn for the true significance of the text.

Swami Rama Bharati, a yogi raised in the cave monasteries of Uttar Pradesh, explains. "A human being is miserable if he fails to unfold his inner potentials. In order to do this he must purify the ego and surrender it to the higher reality. The ego is very useful in helping you to function in the world, but it's not very useful as far as deeper happiness is concerned. The ego is that which separates you from the reality, from the truth, from the ultimate source." The ego is Mahisha. Mahisha's legions include spitefulness, pettiness, untruthfulness and miserliness. His six chief commanders, according to the yoga tradition, are desire, anger, arrogance, attachment, greed and self-centeredness.

"Acknowledge your weak points, let the power of discrimination counsel your ego, and make a strong resolution to overcome your weaknesses," Swami Rama continues. "Remind yourself that you are on the path of inner purification and self-discovery. This path requires great courage. Stand firm during this internal battle and support your *Atman* (your Higher Self), even at the cost of dismantling the ego and all its retinue.

"Once ego surrenders itself to the highest Truth, you have attained victory, and spiritual illumination is yours. Soon after the victory over the ego, all other virtues such as humility, love, selflessness, compassion and kindness, spontaneously unfold. When these virtues blossom, a human being becomes a saint." Or, as the *Chandi* puts it, the demi-gods, the healthful, helpful forces within ourselves, resume their rightful roles in life.

The great 19th century Kriya Yoga master Lahiri Mahasaya was said never to leave his house without a copy of the *Chandi* in his bag. "Durga," Lahiri explained, "is the Self, the Divine Mother which is seen in this physical body in between the eyebrows in a radiant light, in the form of the Goddess of the World."

As human awareness is lifted up the *chakras* from the bottom of the spine to above the top of the skull during the process of kundalini yoga, the purifying power of consciousness encounters tiers of inner demons ranging from childishness to megalomania, self-deprecation to violent self-destructiveness, self-delusion to schizophrenia. Each weapon in Durga's hands represents another tool with which the focused attention of an aspirant can combat these unhealthy energies. Durga's weapons include self-discipline, chanting of sacred mantras, selfless service, honest self-examination, prayer, devotion, cheerfulness, and meditation.

If Durga represents the ever victorious Higher Self, and Mahisha is the ego continually seeking to elude the transformative power of the divine force within, who is Medhas, the sage who reveals the truth about the Goddess to King Suratha and the merchant Samadhi? Shree Maa of Kamakhya, one of the most respected contemporary saints of North India, chants the entire *Chandi* every day. While I was visiting the temple to the Divine Mother where Shree Maa lives, she explained the mystery of Medhas to me. "In

Sanskrit there is a distinction between *buddhi* and *medha*. *Buddhi* means the intellect and *medha* means the intellect illuminated by love. When you have a loving intellect full of joy, full of inspiration, then you are the sage Medhas, the intellect of love.

"You must invite a *bhava*—a divine attitude—into your life. Do you remember the myth in which Tara, the Divine Mother, leaves her husband Jupiter because he is so dry and dull? He represents the *buddhi.* She tells him, 'I need some *bhava.* I am going to the home of the Moon because he is filled with devotion.'" Tara ultimately returned to Jupiter, but only after he propitiated her with tears and sincere emotion.

"In the West students are used to memorizing things for examinations," Shree Maa continued. "When they go into spiritual life they think, 'I'll learn it all from books,' and do the practices from their intellect, not from their heart. They haven't realized the objective is to illuminate your wisdom with *bhakti,* divine love.

"The Divine Mother has two breasts from which she nourishes her children. From the left comes devotion and from the right comes wisdom. Every woman should know that. The intellect alone is not enough nourishment to raise a healthy child. If we have a cold and dull spiritual practice, we have to light it up with flames of devotion.

"Have you heard about the time the Bengali saint Ramakrishna visited the headquarters of the famous political party called the Brahmo Samaj? They were discussing philosophy and cosmology. Ramakrishna stood in the middle of the hall and said, 'Why are you talking about the Moon and the Sun and the planets? Why aren't you calling out to the Divine Mother, the one who made the stars?' He started crying, 'Mother! Mother! Mother!' and went into a state of union with the Supreme.

"The leader of the Brahmo Samaj looked very sad and admitted, 'All my life I have studied the scriptures and sat for meditation, but still I haven't achieved Self-realization. This saint doesn't care to read. All he does is call out to the Mother with pure love, and immediately she wraps him in her arms!'"

Surat is Sanskrit for "attention" and *samadhi* means "continuous one-pointed concentration." When the *Chandi* says King Suratha and the merchant Samadhi lost their position and wealth, it reminds us that our focus has been diverted from our Higher Self, the truth within. It is the sage Medhas, or intelligence infused with divine love, that redirects our awareness to our inner essence.

Shree Maa signaled to Swami Satyananda, sitting nearby. Like Shree Maa and many other Hindu devotees, he also chants the *Chandi* daily. Always delighted to talk about the Divine Mother, the swami elaborated, "There are nine forms of Durga, the Divine Mother, in the *Chandi*. First is the Goddess of Inspiration, second is the Goddess of Sacred Study, third is the Goddess of Spiritual Practice, fourth the Goddess of Inner Refinement, fifth the Goddess who Nurtures Divinity. Sixth is She who Makes Us Completely Pure, seventh the Great Surrender of the Darkness of Duality, eighth She who Makes Us One with Radiant Light, ninth the Granter of Perfection. These are the names of the nine Durgas united in succession in the path of perfection, given from the beginning of time. In the path of material life these nine forces take us to the culmination of our goals."

"And we find these Durgas inside ourselves?" I asked hesitantly.

"Yes! At every point in time we can ask ourselves, 'Which Durga am I illuminating right now? Am I the Goddess of inspiration or am I the teacher of sacred knowledge? Am I performing my spiritual practice? Am I surrendering the darkness of my egotism? Am I illuminating the great radiant light?' These are questions we'll ask ourselves all through the day."

Clearly, the *Chandi* is more than a "bizarre and violent" tribal tale to Hindus. For them it is the story of an inner battle—their inner battle—and finding the capacity to surrender the Mahisha in themselves to Durga's purifying power is their inner victory.

CONQUERING POWER

But there is still one more episode in the *Chandi,* and for Westerners it is perhaps the most relevant of all. This section poses the question, What would happen if the Mother of the Universe, the all conquering primordial power, were to get angry? Really angry?

The conflict described in the *Chandi* repeats itself every day and every hour as the best in us wrestles with the worst. It is a battle each generation takes up anew. And as Medhas, the sage of loving intellect, continued the story, two new adversaries had arisen to challenge the Mother of the Universe. Hearing that a woman of breathtaking beauty was sitting at the top of a nearby mountain, the demon lords Sumbha and Nisumbha desired to possess her. Often when individuals first encounter the divine power in themselves, seated in the *chakra* at the top of the head, their first thought is to use its intuition and other psychic powers for their personal gain.

The demon lords sent their henchmen Chanda and Munda to attack the Goddess on the mountain, hoping to misuse the limitless spiritual abilities of the Higher Self. Recognizing their ignoble intention, the Goddess became extremely angry. Durga's beautiful face, usually luminously serene, began to darken. Then something unimaginably terrifying occurred. The Mother of the Universe, the source of all matter and energy in the cosmos, *frowned*. From the Goddess's knit eyebrows sprang a form more horrible than anything the demons could have imagined in their most distorted nightmares: Kali Ma!

Gaunt and frenzied, with thin pendulous breasts, sunken eyes, and a lolling tongue hanging from her blood stained mouth, Kali burst from the forehead of Durga. Ornamented with a necklace of human bones and wielding a staff topped with a skull, Kali fell upon Chanda, Munda, and their entire army, throwing the petrified demons into her voracious mouth. Because she devoured Chanda and Munda, Kali is also known as Chamunda or Chandika, heroine of the *Chandi*.

More demons were sent to assault the Goddess. The most awful was Rakta Bija, impossible to defeat. Each time Durga wounded him, every drop of his blood, splattering on the ground, turned into a clone of himself. The harder Durga and the army of demi-goddesses she projected from herself fought, the more demons sprang up around them. Finally Durga signalled to Kali. Extending her tongue, Mother Kali caught every drop of Rakta Bija's blood before it reached the earth. Durga slew him at last and Kali gulped down his body. Our unhealthful desires and negative thoughts must be caught before they have a chance to take root in the fertile ground of our subconscious, where they multiply maniacally and take over our lives.

Finally the demon kings Sumbha and Nisumbha themselves

attacked. Watching them approach, Mother Kali shrieked with laughter, and leaping upwards slapped the sky with her hands. Soon Sumbha lay dead and Kali raced over to feast on his corpse.

All the demons had perished except Nisumbha himself, who stood surrounded by legions of feminine power. "This is no fair!" he cried out. "I'm completely outnumbered! There are too many of you!"

Durga smiled. "In all this universe, only I exist. Where do you imagine you see anything other than myself?" As Durga spoke these words, Kali and the other warrioresses merged back into her, the Supreme Self.

But Nisumbha did not grasp the teaching and merge himself back into the Goddess as well. Still the sense of "I-ness" that separates us from our mystical unity with the Divine Mother struggled against the all-devouring power of the Goddess. Still some part of him believed he could control her.

Nisumbha never had a chance. Every arrow he fired at her, every discus he hurled, she snapped with an arrow of her own before it even got near her. Reaching out, she pulled the bow from his hands and snapped it in two between her fingers. Nisumbha tried to wrestle with the Goddess but she threw him to the ground and ran her spear through his heart.

The stormy sky cleared, the rivers resumed their normal courses, and innocent young girls danced with happiness as the sun came out of hiding from behind the clouds. The last source of conflict had fallen, and peace and harmony blanketed the glistening, grateful world.

Westerners seem to find Kali, that lethal projection of Durga's fury, the most fascinating of all the Hindu goddesses. The dark Mother embodies everything about God that makes us uncomfortable. Kali is naked because she is literally stark reality. When all our illusions are stripped away, what remains is the unceasing maelstrom of nature: continual change, constant loss, and inevitable death. The Goddess always wins. There is no real contest.

What many Westerners have such a difficult time understanding is that Hindus love this Goddess. At every Kali shrine I visited in India, Hindus danced and sang and wept with loving devotion. In one of her hands Kali Ma holds the blade with which she slashes everything out of us that is less than divine. In her second hand she holds up her trophy, the severed head of our egotism. But look more closely because with her third hand she signals us, "Don't be afraid!"And with her fourth, she reaches out to bless and protect us.

The forces of nature, those that seal our destiny and send disease and sorrow and death and decay, are the same forces that bring us into being and nurture us. They are also the very same forces which give *moksha,* enlightenment. Like Nisumbha, the part of us which resists the reality that all of us are fundamentally one, that we are all united with spirit and nature as one seamless divine whole, we wrestle with the Goddess. The *Chandi* says Durga allowed Nisumbha to wrestle "for a long time." Many of us can no doubt relate to Nisumbha's frustration at his inability to make the Divine Mother obey his will. When she doesn't immediately answer our prayers we sometimes get aggravated too. Yet at every stage of the struggle she fosters the highest and best in us, till the clouds of our selfish desires and delusions break up, and our inner sun begins to shine, illuminating our lives and the lives of those around us.

Kali is the one Hindu Goddess who's been widely accepted by Western feminists, nature worshipers, and Goddess fans. Their interpretation of what Kali represents is so radically different from the Hindu understanding that it's sometimes hard to imagine we're talking about the same Goddess. New Age Western women tend to look at the goddesses of other times and different cultures as convenient tools for us to use in our psychological vivisection of our personalities, and to emulate if we so choose. Rampaging Kali is seen as an emblem of women's rage against patriarchy (Durga and Kali slay only males). Embodying her means giving ourselves permission to vent our fury.

To the Hindu, the Goddess is not an archetype or a tool for psychological self analysis. She is a living reality more real, in a sense, than ourselves. The Divine Mother is the source of all archetypes, indeed the source of everything in all dimensions of being. Many women in India worship Kali, but they're not worshiping her to get in touch with their anger. Although she is born of the desire to right wrong, Kali is not about vengeance. Because she's coming from Durga, from a level of consciousness which is completely centered—which is *the* center—she's the source of all strength, lying far beyond the grip of anger. So she fights and wins all battles in life without losing her composure. She controls the power of anger—it doesn't control her—it's just an energy emanating from her at her command, used at the service of her limitless wisdom.

When we are angry we're not in touch with Kali; in fact, we're entertaining a condition that Kali is set to destroy because she's the purifying power of consciousness and doesn't tolerate demonic emotions or impulses. Anger sets us up against someone or something we perceive as an enemy. And when we perceive anything as other than our Highest Self, as other than the Goddess, then we are in the grips of an illusion. The yogis call this *avidya,* limited understanding. The limitations of our mind and senses prevent us from seeing the whole picture, the fundamental unity of all things. The *Vedas* say that "seers see all beings in the Self, and the Self in all beings; therefore they hate no one." They perceive themselves and everyone else as emanations of the Divine Mother.

As I traveled through South India, I was incredibly impressed by the work Ammachi, a contemporary saint from Kerala, was doing to improve the condition of women there, providing homes and education and vocational training for widows and battered wives. Both she and Shree Maa of Kamakhya are teaching women how to perform religious rituals that for generations only men have been allowed to do. Although they are fixing things Indian women are angry about, Ammachi and Shree Maa are not angry women. They understand that Kali's energy is not anger—it's conquering power. So they come from a center within themselves of loving harmony, and through that truly divine force they're overcoming patriarchal institutions and abuses. When you're sitting in their presence you see the divine at work, you directly perceive Kali's power.

The Western perspective is that we need to get in touch with and learn to express our anger; the Shakta perspective is that we need to acknowledge our anger and then let it go. Anger does not harm the person or institution we fume against, though it sends biotoxins coursing through our own veins. The one correct use for anger is the one Kali shows us: using it to motivate ourselves to fight injustice. But until we sense the value of the space beyond anger, allowing ourselves to be dominated by destructive emotions places us in the camp of Chanda and Munda, not at the side of the ever victorious Goddess.

"Kali never gets angry," Ammachi insists. She has dedicated a shrine to Kali at her ashram in Amritapuri, South India. "Even if Kali seems furious, her motive is born out of pure love and her goal is the purification of the disciple. When we yell at a cow saying, 'Go away!' when it eats the leaves of a young coconut palm, we have the same attitude of fierceness. The cow will not run away if we lovingly tell it to go. It needs a certain show of anger. Likewise, the Mother is roaring and killing the ego through the manifestation of Kali.

"If we worship the fierce aspect of the Divine Mother while knowing and understanding the essential principle behind it, there is no harm. Our attitude should be that Kali is the absolute pure being, that she is the Supreme Power and that she is everything. Some, however, worship Kali considering her only as a fierce goddess who kills enemies, but those who worship her in that manner will have the same fiery nature. Quarrels and conflicts will occur in their houses, which will cause harm to them who worship in that way. In fact, that is the wrong conception and the wrong way to worship her.

"Look at the fierce form of Kali. Kali is the destroyer of the ego. Because a true seeker wants to be free from the ego, he will love this aspect of the Divine Mother. Surrendering to Kali or what she represents, a true devotee will happily offer his head to her in order to add one more head to Kali's garland of skulls.

"A devotee who is still attached to possessions and wealth, and to honor and position, will greatly fear this aspect of the divine. He will never keep a picture of her in his house. He's afraid that Kali will destroy everything dear to him. He thinks she will kill his ego and that without his ego he cannot exist. An ordinary devotee wants to keep his ego, whereas a true devotee wants to die to this ego so that he can live in divine consciousness and pure, innocent love."

KALI'S SAINTS

The worship of Mother Kali is enormously popular in India. Perhaps no two figures in the last three centuries have been more significant in promoting her worship than Ramprasad and

Ramakrishna, both deeply beloved saints of Bengal. Their stories may be helpful in understanding how Hindus relate to Kali Ma.

First let us turn back to the 18th century, where we find Ramprasad, as usual, in deep trouble. His supervisor had repeatedly warned that if he couldn't keep the business accounts straight, he couldn't keep his job. And once again his boss had checked the ledger and found that poetry, not figures, filled the columns. This time, Ramprasad was being called in to face the general manager.

Ramprasad had never been a good provider for his wife and four children. His father, a successful Ayurvedic physician, had expected the boy to follow his profession, but Ramprasad showed little aptitude for medicine. In fact, after his meeting a tantric scholar named Agama Vagisha, he showed little inclination for anything except meditation, and his father had to assist him and his growing family financially for years. The old doctor's death left Ramprasad destitute; he reluctantly moved his family south to the Calcutta area where he hoped his knowledge of Persian and Hindi, the major commercial languages of North India in the mid 1700s, would help him find some kind of work. He finally found a job as the clerk in charge of a company's account books, earning a modest salary of 30 rupees per month. He did not do well.

It wasn't that he was lazy, Ramprasad tried to explain to his exasperated wife. It was because there was a woman he couldn't get off his mind. He was on fire, he was being consumed. His wife didn't think much of her competition for Ramprasad's affections: the mad, naked, black-skinned goddess Kali who drank blood and stomped on the corpse of the great God Shiva. Kali represented the efforts of spiritual aspirants to embrace the puissant, uncontrolled, destructive aspect of the Divine Mother. Ramprasad reveled in the turbulent, bizarre facets of Kali, accepting these as legitimate expressions of a mad, reeling, sometimes very harsh and unsympathetic universe. He approached the overwhelming and fearsome energies of the cosmos like a naive child trusting that the mother who brought him into the world would continue to care for him.

Ramprasad understood the tremendous inner significance of this terrifying Goddess. He wrote:

> You shine in deepest darkness, Mother,
> so yogis worship you in dark caves.

They find in your limitless darkness
    limitless peace.
Who are you, Mother,
    clothed with nothingness,
    glowing in the deepest recesses of my mind?
Your frenzied laughter terrifies,
    while your love, like lightning from a black cloud,
    shocks the world with light.

Ramprasad's wife was only gradually becoming reconciled to her fate: to be married to a man in love with a Goddess. It can be inspiring to hear about historical figures like Chaitanya or Mira Bai, saints beside themselves with love for God, but to live with a real life mystic is something altogether different! Once she had even angrily remonstrated with the statue of Kali in the family's tiny shrine room: "Mother, my husband's devotional songs do not put food in our children's mouths!"

And now, haughty with indignation, the supervisor placed the ruined account book before Durgacharan Mitra, the owner of the business. Slowly Mitra paged through the ledger, reading lines like:

Mother Kali, you dwell in cremation grounds
    so I've made my heart a burning pit
    where you can dance.
One desire burns in the conflagration of my life:
    to watch your blazing dance!
I've smeared my body with the ashes of the dead
    to appeal to you.
Lord Shiva lies beneath your feet
    gaping up at your dance.
I sit here waiting
    in my funeral pyre,
    looking for you
    with eyes closed.

When Mitra looked up again Ramprasad was startled to see his employer so deeply moved that tears streamed down his cheeks. Then, looking directly into Ramprasad's eyes, Mitra announced, "You're fired!"

History does not record the thoughts that filled Ramprasad's mind as he turned away to face again the despair of abject poverty. Perhaps he remembered the words from one of his own compositions, complaining to Kali of his pennilessness:

> Mother, how peculiarly your devotee is dressed!
> He's so poor, he doesn't own a single piece of cloth.

Then—"Just a moment!" Mitra called after him. "My boy, you were not brought into this world to be an accountant. Go home and devote yourself to spiritual practices. Don't worry about supporting your family; I'll send you an allowance of 30 rupees every month. The writing of your hallowed hand has sanctified my account book, and I'll treasure it forever."

Durgacharan Mitra was a successful merchant of his time, a pillar of his community. Nevertheless, his name would long since have faded from history, except that in this moment of luminous clarity he immortalized himself by becoming the patron of Ramprasad, one of the greatest mystical poets of all time.

Ramprasad's unique charm as a spiritual poet was the unnerving intimacy with which he addressed divine being. When life dealt him a low blow, he didn't hesitate to let the Goddess know he expected better.

> May I ask where you learned
>   to treat your children so badly?
> If this is how you want to behave,
>   you have no right to call yourself a mother!

Because he thought of God as his mother, fear and awe did not get in the way of Ramprasad's relationship with Spirit. Reality might be difficult, even terrifying at times, but she was also his source, his sustenance and his destiny.

One morning Ramprasad was heading down to the Ganges to perform his morning worship. He used to walk to the river spontaneously singing the praises of the Goddess, and people would come from all over to listen to his divinely inspired songs. One morning a striking looking woman stopped him and asked, "Ramprasad—would you please sing one of your devotional *bhajans* for me?"

Ramprasad was annoyed at being interrupted on his way to do

his morning meditation and answered, "Not now! I'm on my way to worship the Goddess. I'll sing for you when I return." So he waded out into the river and started crying, "Oh Mother, when will you appear to me? For years I have called to you, begging for a vision of you! Please come to me! I yearn to behold you! I weep with longing for the sight of your holy feet!"

After several hours of this he marched back up toward his village, and at the spot where the woman had stopped him earlier he found a message scrawled across the wall of a temple. "My darling Ramprasad, you have been crying to me for so many years, today I could bear it no more. I had to appear before you and assuage your grief. I am very sorry this was not a convenient time."

This story struck me very forcefully. I lived in an ashram for many years, where we residents would dutifully chant our mantras, stand on our heads, and run around 20 hours a day doing our spiritual busywork. Sometimes it seemed we were so busy trying to reach the Divine Mother that we didn't realize we were already in her lap. This lesson was not lost on Ramprasad either. He spent the rest of his life striving to shift his consciousness out of the expectation-ridden time continuum into the eternal present, the true abode of the Divine Mother.

Another famous legend relates that one morning as Ramprasad and his daughter were mending their fence, the young girl became bored with the tedious work and slipped off to play. Sitting on the other side of the fence, Ramprasad didn't notice her leave, yet from the opposite side of the fence someone kept handing him the cord he needed each time he reached up for it. Later when he thanked his daughter, she shamefacedly confessed it was not she who had helped him.

Ramprasad could find no one who admitted patiently handing him cord all day. It finally occurred to him that while he had been working, his mind intently focused on the Divine Mother, she herself had stood by doling cord! Ramprasad noted that all devotees at one time or another have had the experience of an invisible hand of grace supporting their greatest as well as their least endeavors, when they were aware of it and sometimes even when they were not.

Ramprasad devoted most of his life to intense yogic practice, turning his love into wisdom and his wisdom into realization. Yoga philosophy teaches that the divine is formless—it is not limited by any name, gender, or any other image or quality we project upon it. Nevertheless, Ramprasad's life demonstrates that a personal relationship with the Goddess can provide the inspiration which makes Self-realization possible.

This lesson was taken to heart by another Bengali devotee who lived in Calcutta a century later: Ramakrishna, one of the greatest Indian saints of the modern era. Ramakrishna was also a devotee of the "mad mother Kali." He and his disciples would sit for hours singing Ramprasad's ecstatic songs to the Divine Mother.

Once a devotee asked Ramakrishna to describe how Kali acts in the world. "She plays with the world in various ways," the master smiled. "Before the creation of the sun and stars, when there was nothing but darkness anywhere, Mother Kali was formless, her limitless power merged in Supreme Consciousness.

"There is another aspect of Kali, loved and worshipped in many Hindu households because she grants boons and dispels fear. Still another aspect, Kali the Protectress, is worshiped during catastrophes like earthquakes, floods, drought, epidemics and famines. Kali of the Cremation Grounds lives by the burning pyres with ghosts and scavenging animals who eat human flesh. Blood oozes from her mouth, a garland of human heads hangs around her neck, and a belt of human arms—representing all our accomplishments—is tied around her waist. She is the power of destruction embodied.

"At the end of the cycle of manifestation, when the universe is destroyed, she gathers the seeds of karma left over from the last creation and keeps them in her pot, like a housewife collecting herbs and vegetables to make stew! Then she creates a new universe and pervades it with her limitless power. She's just like a spider: the spider weaves a web out of its own belly and then lives in it.

"A spider captures and devours prey in its web," Ramakrishna continued. "Just so Mother Kali captures us in her web of *maya*. With a twinkle in her eye she tells us, 'Go ahead, enjoy life!' This sounds appealing so we rush out and entangle ourselves in worldliness, in sensuality and greed, and then she has us. We're caught!

"You see, the Divine Mother is always playful. And she always insists on having her own way. All this universe is her game, filling her with delight. But just as she is the cause of all our bondage, she is also the source of freedom. She can free anyone she likes. Through her grace she allows the mind to turn inward toward herself. Then the soul becomes devoted to her beautiful lotus feet."

"So we must completely renounce the world in order to realize her?" a devotee hazarded.

The master laughed. "Why renounce anything? You're fine the way you are, following the middle path like molasses, which is half solid and half liquid!" Smiling joyfully Ramakrishna elaborated, "There is nothing wrong with living in the world. But if you want to be happy, you must constantly turn your attention back to God. Fulfill your obligations in the world with one hand, but with the other hand hang on to the Divine Mother. After your responsibilities are complete, hang on with both hands!

"People cry jugs of tears for their lovers and children. Who cries for God? Go off by yourself from time to time and weep for the Divine Mother. It will do you a world of good.

"They say Mother Kali is black, that she has a very dark complexion. This is how she appears from the distance, but when you get closer you'll see this isn't so. The sky looks blue from the distance but up close it's completely clear. The ocean also looks blue until you lift out a handful of it and find it's clear too. Just so, Kali is actually transparent and formless."

Because the Divine Mother's real nature is transparent, she is very difficult to perceive. For the sake of interacting with those of us who haven't cultivated the subtle vision necessary to see the unseen, she assumes forms like Sarasvati or Isis, Mary or Quan Yin, Pele or Athena, Freya or Inanna. These forms dramatically embody the deeper reality of her true being. Kali may be her most dramatic embodiment of all.

DURGA'S BLESSING

At the conclusion of the *Chandi*, the gods celebrated Durga's victory, calling out to her:

> O Goddess of Light, you who unfailingly remove the distress
>   of those souls who take refuge in you with full faith,
> Sovereign Empress of the entire universe,

please safeguard the world!
You are the ocean of being from which the cosmos pours.
You quench the thirst of parched souls
    with the ambrosia of everlasting life.
Though you delude the world,
    it is in your hands to remove your *maya,*
    granting everlasting freedom!

We bow to you for you graciously protect
    the weak and the oppressed.
O Chandika, may your sword,
    smeared with the blood of unwholesome motivations,
    protect us from disease and calamity.
Wherever there are demons, poison snakes,
    criminals and other enemies, wildfire and other dangers,
    wherever there is terror, you stand guard.
The whole universe bows to you in adoration!
O Mother, be gracious!
Just as you rescued us from the demons today,
    please promise to save us
    whenever we call out to you,
    in all times to come!

In response, the Goddess promised:

Whenever there is oppression arising out of evil forces
    I shall descend into the three worlds and destroy it,
    when you call out to me with hearts full of faith.
Whoever contemplates my saving grace
    with full concentration and loving devotion,
    I will relieve of disease and misfortune;
    they need fear neither weapons nor fire nor floods.
I will never abandon that abode
    where prayers to me are offered continually.
Listening to the tales of my deeds, one becomes fearless
    and is unaffected by evil dreams or painful planetary cycles;
    friendships are renewed and family welfare is assured.
Hearing of my deeds and contemplating my divine nature
    removes sins and grants everlasting joy!

Having spoken thus, the Goddess of infinite prowess vanished into thin air!

"And so the Goddess, fulfilling her promise, manifests in the world again and again for the protection of the good," the sage Medhas concluded as the *Chandi* draws to a close. "We have only to cry out to her from the depths of our hearts, offering her our pure love."

King Suratha and the merchant Samadhi were so inspired by the story of the *Chandi* that they devoted the next three years of their lives exclusively to lovingly worshiping Durga. Due to the tremendous merit earned from this worship, King Suratha won back his kingdom, not only for his present incarnation but for many lives to come. The merchant Samadhi, however, chose another course. When Durga appeared to him at the end of his three year retreat, he asked for the spiritual knowledge which removes sorrow and delusion forever. Beaming with delight, the Mother of the Universe granted his prayer.

When the long-suffering and truly virtuous king Yudhisthira, though vastly outnumbered, set out to battle the rapacious prince Duryodhana in the cataclysmic war chronicled in the *Mahabharata,* he remembered the Divine Mother's promise in the *Chandi* and how she had helped Rama conquer the tyrant Ravanna. Filled with devotion, he paused to worship Mother Durga, hoping to win her grace for the upcoming struggle. He chanted her thousand names and appealed to her with a famous heartfelt prayer, adapted in part below. For centuries Hindus have recited this prayer before facing their personal battles.

Durga gave Yudhisthira the victory.

Durga Stotram:

Prayer for Victory

Slayer of the demon Mahisha,
 the gods themselves worship you
 for the sake of the protection of the universe.
You give victory in battle
 for you are victory itself.
Goddess, blazing with light, be kind to me!

Show mercy in my hour of darkness!
Grant me conquering power!

Mother Kali, there is no limit to your power
    or to your grace!
The Creator of the world propitiates you
    with all the cosmic powers
    who beg you to lighten their burdens.
They call you by the name "Durga"
    because you save your children from difficulties.
Mother, you are our sole refuge
    when we are attacked by robbers,
    and when we cross the storming sea!
In the deepest wilderness,
    those who remember you are never lost!

When worshiped by your devotees,
    you remove their ignorance, their bondage,
    their fear, disease, and threat of death.
You protect their children and their goods.
I who have lost everything appeal for your help,
    bowing to you reverently, Mother of the Gods.
Protect me, lotus-eyed savioress!
I am fighting for the truth;
    protect me with all the power of truth!
O Durga, shelter me in your wide lap.
You who are ever loving and merciful to devotees,
    please help!

The Goddess of Victory appeared before Yudhisthira
and lovingly addressed him:

O mighty king, fighting the forces of unrighteousness,
    the victory will soon be yours.
You will become an emperor, ruling justly.
Due to your goodness, for your people
    it will be as if the earth had lost its thorns.
I grant you, and your family also, joy and health.

Those who, like you, worship me sincerely
    will be freed from the results of their bad karma.
I will give them beauty, wealth, stature, healthy children
    and long, happy lives.
Those who invoke me, as you have,
    will be safe in the battlefield,
    in the jungle, in the desert,
    in the mountains, and on the sea.
Every success I will bestow
    on those who remember me and your loving prayer.

Having arranged for the victory of Yudhisthira, the Goddess Durga dematerialized before the good king's grateful eyes.

5

Lalita
The Goddess as Consciousness

Homage to the Absolute Reality,
the source and embodiment of bliss,
the Supreme Consciousness,
she who is both the magnificent image of the universe
and the mirror of pure awareness
in which this dazzling reflection appears!
Tripura Rahasya II, i, 1.

Most of us in the West aren't used to thinking of "reality" as something conscious, much less as something female, yet this insight is the epiphany of Tantra. My own first encounter with the living reality Shaktas call the Goddess occurred when I was 14 years old. I was alone at home, walking across the dining room. Without a glimmer of warning, between lifting my foot up and putting it back down—literally in the space of a step, in less than a breath—my consciousness suddenly no longer ended at the boundary of my skin. My awareness, the very essence of my being, surged outward, encompassing the air around me, the walls, the building, and continued to expand explosively. I am not speaking metaphorically. This was completely real, my actual, literal experience. I was no longer merely my body. I was *everything*.

The ecstacy I experienced in that instant is beyond the furthest capacity of words to describe. In that blink of an eye I realized—absolutely, to my very core—that everything is alive, that the innermost quintessence of reality is pure self-existent being, conscious and inconceivably blissful. That there is no difference between you and me. That there is no difference between God and us.

Nothing in my life had prepared me for this experience. My birth religion had taught me that I am utterly separate from God—in my first 14 years the concept that all of life is a unified, conscious whole had never occurred to me. The experience wasn't drug induced; I've never used drugs in my life.

What happened that day was impossible, inconceivable. Yet that explosion of awareness was incontrovertibly the most real thing that ever happened to me, and I needed to understand it. Even more desperately, I needed to find the way back. The experience had lasted only a moment, yet the instant my all pervading consciousness collapsed back into my body had been a horrible shock. Suddenly my body became a prison cell. I now saw my mind and personality—which I had previously considered most fundamentally me—as the faintest tip of an iceberg of being as deep and broad as the universe itself. I no longer believed that God and I were eternally separate. I experienced that I had been together with God forever, that there was absolutely no difference between us. This was not a theology anyone had taught me, but a spontaneous, indisputable realization. Perhaps that is why the Hindus call this type of experience Sanatana Dharma, the eternal truth. If every Hindu were to perish today, tomorrow the truth would be rediscovered. Somewhere someone would spontaneously awaken.

In the Goddess tradition of India truth itself is called Shiva, and the living experience of truth is called Shakti. In one of the major Goddess lineages the perfect unity of Shiva and Shakti or self-existent reality and its ecstatic self-recognition is called Maha Tripura Sundari, the Supreme Goddess or, literally, "the Supreme Beauty who dwells in three cities." The three cities are the physical, subtle and causal planes of existence, or on the human level, the physical, mental and spiritual components of our being. Often she is simply called Lalita, "she who plays." The borderless cosmos is her playground. We are her toys. At every moment, whether we have the eyes to see it or not, we are totally immersed in and surrounded by and filled with and guided by Supreme Beauty. *Satyam shivam sundaram:* "Absolute Truth is Ultimate Good is Supreme Beauty."

In the Goddess tradition therefore, the sages are those pure souls who remain in a state of constant delight. They do not experience ugliness anywhere. It is not that they don't recognize the sorrow and evil the rest of us see all around us—they see through it. Suffering is part of the play. In theater, everyone knows the greatest dramas are the tragedies.

I sometimes get tired of suffering, myself. War, crime, social injustice, disease, death, friends betraying each other, children unloved: often it gets hard to see the beauty. I don't want to be the Goddess's "toy," a "victim" of the inexorable processes of nature. Watching my husband's struggle with cancer has left me with a deep distaste for the merciless mechanics of the natural world. In the Shakta tradition they say that when you get really tired of being a bit player in a cosmic melodrama where you don't know the script, then it's time to get to know the producer, to get to know Lalita. When I was 14 years old the Goddess walked through my house and the hem of her skirt grazed my heart. In that instant of unimaginable grace I directly experienced her living presence, a tantalizing reminder that life is more than I see before my eyes and that I am more than this body. But that was the last stroke of *shaktipat* (literally, "downpour of enlightening energy") she graced me with. In the yogic tradition it's said that these flashes of cosmic consciousness are not actually rare, but they aren't stable. For all my prayers and pleading and tears, that supremely beautiful instant of Self-recognition has never reoccurred. The Goddess will tease you with a spontaneous hint of her/your divine nature, but if you want to experience it again, she makes you work for it.

Working for it is called *sadhana* in Sanskrit, "spiritual practice." *Sadhana* begins with Ten Commitments, a set of do's and don'ts that forms the foundation of yogic life.

1. Don't harm others.
2. Don't be dishonest.
3. Don't take anything that isn't yours.
4. Don't overindulge in sensuality.
5. Don't be greedy.
6. Do cultivate physical cleanliness, emotional purity and mental clarity.
7. Do be content with what your karma has brought you.
8. Do discipline yourself.
9. Do study your psychological and spiritual makeup.
10. Do love the Supreme Being with your whole being.

In India, Goddess *sadhana*, like most forms of spiritual practice coming out of the Hindu tradition, is rooted in asceticism and nonattachment. These are not popular values in today's New Age spirituality, probably because contemporary Westerners have completely lost sight of the underlying purpose of asceticism. In the context of Shaktism, self-denial does not mean self-mortification, it means self-discipline with the goal of plumbing deeper aspects of oneself concealed beneath the daily concerns of "getting and spending."

Suppose you grew up on a diet of network television. With only a few exceptions, most of the TV shows you watched were of pretty poor quality. Now suppose someone introduces you to satellite TV. Suddenly a whole new universe of channels opens up for you. You gain access to the finest movies, top sports events, and the best in cultural and educational programming. But in order to change over to the satellite stations, you have to flip the switch that shuts off your connection to network television.

Asceticism is turning off the switch which keeps us hooked up to the programming fed to us by our five senses. Withdrawing the mind from external distractions, we turn our focus inward, and suddenly a new universe of channels becomes available. Through meditation we learn to tune our minds to subtler frequencies, to higher orders of reality inherent in subtler dimensions. Most people are content with network television, but spiritual aspirants are those few who are willing to do the inner work required to tune in to the cosmic broadcast of the saints, celestial entities, and Divine Being itself.

Nonattachment is similarly misunderstood in the West. We often think being nonattached means not caring, despite the example of India's "nonattached" saints, who are the most loving people on the planet. What distinguishes these saints from the rest of us is that they love completely, without the least concern whether they get any credit for it. They love not for what they might receive in return; whether anyone loves them back or appreciates their selfless activities is of no concern. They broadcast compassion to everyone and everything without discriminating who is bad or who is good, who is rich or who is poor, just as the Sun radiates its light on everyone freely and equally. Unconditional love means no strings attached.

Being nonattached in the Shakta tradition means being free to love everyone fully in every moment in time. Having rid themselves of favoritism and expectations, India's saints subsume their personalities into the core of their being, into limitless bliss which radiates into our world in the form of selfless love.

STEP LADDER TO THE GODDESS

WARNING: You are now leaving Western consensus reality. The Shakta universe lies ahead. The masters of the Goddess tradition perceive the world very differently than you do. If you have no experience with meditation or have never spent time in an Eastern culture, the material which follows may seem challenging. However, if you keep your mind open to the information presented here, your understanding of yourself, the universe, and the Goddess may shift in surprising ways.

In order to understand the subtler channels we begin receiving in meditation, as well as how ascetic practice leads to Tantra and how Tantra leads beyond asceticism, it is necessary to understand one of the most central tenets of Tantra, the 37 *tattvas* or cosmic levels. Much of today's confusion about higher states of consciousness exists because these categories have been forgotten. Yet it is the ladder of the *tattvas* which leads us to the feet of Lalita, the Supreme Goddess. Please be patient for a few pages while I explain how the *tattvas* beautifully reveal who Lalita really is and how spiritual practices work.

Western translators often use the term "element" for *tattva*, lacking a more accurately descriptive English word, but it instantly gives the wrong impression. We were taught in grade school that there are over one hundred elements starting with hydrogen, helium and lithium, and that the distinction between them is the number of protons, neutrons and electrons they contain. When the great minds of another culture tell us there are 37 elements and they start with earth, water, fire, and air, there's a tendency to roll our eyes and dismiss these people as illiterate and superstitious. We completely miss the point. We're too biased toward our own point of view to make an effort to understand the truths the other culture is trying to convey.

THE TANTRIC UNIVERSE

THE GODDESS
37. Maha Tripura Sundari
The One

SUPREME REALITY

35. Shakti	36. Shiva
Infinite Energy	Infinite Consciousness

PURE CREATION

32. Shuddha Vidya	33. Ishvara	34. Sada Shiva
Object/Subject	Subject/Object	Subject = Object

ILLUSION
31. Maya
Capacity to Focus on the Finite

LIMITING CONDITIONS

26. Niyati	27. Kâla	28. Raga	29. Vidya	30. Kalâ
Limits	Limits	Causes	Limits	Limits
Omnipresence	Eternity	Desire	Onmiscience	Omnipotence

SPIRIT
25. Purusha
Individual Soul

MATTER
24. Prakriti
Material Matrix

MIND

21. Manas	22. Ahankara	23. Buddhi
Thought Processes	Self Identity	Judgment

SENSE ORGANS

16. Ghrana	17. Jinva	18. Chakshu	19. Tvak	20. Stotra
Smell	Taste	Sight	Touch	Hearing

ORGANS OF ACTION

11. Payu	12. Upastha	13. Pada	14. Pani	15. Vak
Excreting	Procreating	Locomoting	Handing	Speaking

SUBTLE ELEMENTS

6. Gandha	7. Rasa	8. Rupa	9. Sparsha	10. Shabda
Odor	Flavor	Color	Feeling	Sound

GROSS ELEMENTS

1. Prithivi	2. Apas	3. Agni	4. Vayu	5. Akasha
Solidity	Liquidity	Combustibility	Gaseousness	Spaceousness

The ancient Hindu sages did not smash atoms together in particle accelerators in order to understand the nature of matter, though they did have a sophisticated concept of the atom—called *paramanu* or "smallest particle" in Sanskrit—described in texts like the *Vaisesika Sutra*. What they did instead was categorize the world into elements based on subjective experience. For example, we experience solid stuff and liquid stuff and things in the process of transforming themselves, such as fire. There is gaseous stuff like air and then there's space itself, which although it appears to be empty, according to the yoga masters is actually a substance. (Western physicists have recently begun to share this view as they note subatomic particles appearing to materialize out of a vacuum. The "zero-point energy field" described in quantum mechanics is a close correlate of the ancient *tattva* called space.) These principles represent the first five cosmic elements with which many ancient civilizations were familiar, usually lamely translated as earth, water, fire, air and space or ether.

These five elements also represent the entire length and breadth of our supposedly advanced modern science. From the point of view of the Shaktas, physical matter and its fields represent only a tiny portion of reality as a whole. Western scientists cannot even begin to answer questions such as, "Does human consciousness survive death? Is there a God? How do thoughts affect the body? How does spontaneous healing occur?" because they have not yet begun to explore the other 32 *tattvas* or levels of reality which are subtler than physical matter.

What other categories do we notice in our subjective experience? The first five *tattvas* have internal correlates called *tanmatras,* subtle elements. Outside our bodies, fire burns any flammable object placed in it. A blazing fire vividly imagined in our minds burns just as brightly, yet our skulls aren't singed! Smells, tastes, colors, tactile sensations and sounds are important components of our experience, and are literally the stuff of which dreams are made. Yogis work with this form of "subtle matter" in certain of their concentration exercises, and claim that there are other worlds made of this intangible material. These subtle elements, visible to our mind's eye but not to our physical eyes, comprise rungs 6-10 on the ladder to the Goddess.

Next we note that we have the ability not only to perceive but also to manipulate our bodies and external objects. We can speak, hold things, walk around, procreate and excrete. Rocks cannot do these things. These five types of action compose cosmic categories 11-15.

Of course in order to manipulate objects, we need to be able to perceive them. Categories 16-20 are the five senses themselves: smelling, tasting, seeing, feeling, hearing. Here comes an important point, one which medical experts today have completely missed: the senses are not the same as the five physical sense organs, the eyes, tongue, nose, etc. or the brain. As masters of meditation, the yogis experienced the sensation of leaving their physical bodies as their consciousness appeared to travel unhampered through space. Noting that they could still see and hear in their "mental bodies," the yogis concluded the actual experience of sensation must lie in the subtle body, not its physical counterpart.

Beyond these lies another sensory mechanism, the mind, which is designed to process sense data from the external world, but can be trained to perceive input from inner dimensions of reality as well. The yogis divided the mind into three distinct faculties. There's the part which processes, stores and retrieves information. They called this *manas,* the Sanskrit term cognate with the English word man, "the one who thinks." Next is the mental function which relates information to a particular individual, giving him the sense, "This is my knowledge. This is happening to me." When this part of the mind in unable to express itself in the physical brain, as occasionally happens after particular types of head injuries, a patient is unable to recognize that his arms or legs are part of his own body. This sense of "me-ness" was called *ahankara.* Finally, there's the *buddhi,* an extremely difficult word to render into English, often inadequately translated as intellect or intuition. It is the decision making faculty which weighs alternatives and coordinates appropriate reactions, acting on the basis of the sensory input *manas* supplies. These three components of the mind form rungs 21-23.

As one of the Shakta masters I studied with constantly repeated, "All of the body is in the mind, but not all of the mind is in the body." He insisted that the mind is a psychic organ which operates through a physical nervous system during life, allowing it to easily interact with physical matter. After death (or for yogis, during excursions outside their physical bodies), the mind separates from the physical organism it inhabited, making it much more difficult to interact with the physical world, but much easier to act in the realm of the *tanmatras* or subtle elements. Yogis have demonstrated the distinction between mind and the brain in thoroughly documented laboratory experiments where EEG equipment confirmed that the yogi's brain was in "deep sleep" or even registered a near total lack of electrical activity usually associated with "brain death," and yet the yogi was completely lucid and able to report in detail the events occurring in the lab while he was supposedly unconsciousness. The brain was asleep; the mind was fully awake. Achieving this level of mastery over the nervous system is an important milestone in the yoga tradition.

We have 23 *tattvas* so far. Why did yogis in ancient times categorize the universe in this odd, apparently arbitrary way? It was because they could gauge their spiritual progress by noting which of these *tattvas* filled their field of awareness during meditation. Beginning meditators are usually primarily aware of the pain in their legs or their itchy noses or someone shouting outside. Attention focused on gross external stimuli reflects a fairly low level of meditative depth. As awareness shifts more deeply within, one might perceive a whole sound and light show, splashes of spinning colors and intriguing internal sounds. This indicates a shift from gross to subtle perception as meditation is getting deeper.

Pulling back further from physical and subtle stimuli, one enters what Patanjali (author of the classic *Yoga Sutras)* calls "mental absorption accompanied by bliss," a state of intense inner delight. Before this level, meditation is often hard work. But now awareness is passing out of range of external and internal sense objects (up through *tattva* 20), and only the most refined sensations are experienced. At this point meditation becomes an addictive pleasure. Here the heart goes *vroooom,* bursting open in incredible, indescribable joy. You feel like you're levitating, as if the Goddess is tossing your heart in the air. Mystics of many different religious traditions have described ecstatic spiritual experiences in this state. But the yoga scriptures warn: Okay, enjoy yourself, but don't get stuck at this stage. Make yourself familiar with the experience, then move on.

There are many different states of consciousness one passes through in deep meditation, including "mental absorption accompanied by the feeling of I-ness." At this point one has passed beyond physical and emotional sensations all together. There are no distracting thoughts or images. One simply experiences one's own existence—"I am." Like all deep meditative states this experience is blissful, but at an octave higher than "blissful absorption." The "high pitch" of ecstacy is gone, replaced by a state of deep peace and "I-ness" resulting from intense focus on *tattva* 22, *ahankara* or the sense of selfhood. Powerful orators surreptitiously attempt to place their audience into this type of intense concentration so they can take over the audience members' self-sense and influence their behavior. Entered into passively or involuntarily, this state can lead to hypnotic receptiveness, "mob consciousness," and loss of self-control.

Understanding the *tattvas* is more than an intellectual exercise. For example, it is useful to know that many "psychic" experiences occur at the fairly low level of the *tanmatras* (categories 6-10) while genuine spiritual insight and intuition occur in the subtler aspects of the *buddhi* (category 23). As Patanjali himself emphasizes, the cultivation of spiritual insight is far more productive than the pursuit of psychic powers.

The 24th cosmic category is a big one: *prakriti* or primordial matter (not to be confused with physical matter, which is limited to categories 1-5). This is the eternal matrix from which all the previous 23 components of reality have sprung. It's not matter in the usual Western sense, but is more like an ocean of energy which is the ultimate source not only of the fields we usually think of as energy (gravity, the strong and weak nuclear forces, and electromagnetism) but which is also the source of subtler dimensions of reality than our physical senses can perceive. This ocean is the "primeval waters" mentioned in almost all ancient creation myths including the Bible's. Its waves are always in one of three states: activity, inertia, or equilibrium, symbolized by red, black and white respectively, the colors of the Goddess.

This 24th *tattva* sometimes comes as a shock to Western students, who have been taught to believe their waking level of consciousness represents their immortal soul. According to classical yoga, the mind and personality are material constituents, not spiritual entities. Our thoughts, emotions and perceptions have their base in *prakriti* or primordial matter, not spirit. The mind changes in every moment and ultimately perishes. The "real" Self is the *purusha,* category 25, the inner witness: unchanging, absolute consciousness. The Self is not one's thoughts or feelings or experiences; it merely watches them. Thoughts come and go, the inner Self remains the same. *Purusha* or the Higher Self is completely distinct from matter and never interacts with it. Just as the movie-goer sitting in a theater is not the heroine in the film, but may become completely identified with the heroine's triumphs and tribulations, temporarily forgetting her actual identity as a theater-goer, so when *purusha's* conscious energy illuminates our minds, we experience ourselves as heros or villains, conquerors or victims, in the ceaseless play of nature.

When Buddhist practitioners claim the personality is *sunyata,* empty, they are referring to the fact that the mind is part of *prakriti,* and has no inherent existence beyond the fluctuating, integrated fields of primordial matter. When Hindu practitioners claim that all we are and experience is *neti, neti,* "not this, not this," they mean the Inner Self exists beyond matter, beyond even the mind.

This isn't making sense to you? Hang on just a little longer, and maybe I can show you that you've actually had the experience of this Inner Self though you may not have recognized what it was at the time. You don't understand what this has to do with the Goddess? Friends, we've nearly reached her feet.

ENCOUNTERING THE INNER SELF

Readers savvy to the history of Western philosophy will be reminded of Rene Descartes who in 1641 published a massively influential monograph titled *Meditations.* In it he asked what he could be absolutely sure was real. Could he imagine himself existing if the entire world ceased to exist? Yes, easily. Could he imagine himself existing if his body suddenly disappeared? Actually, yes. But what about his ideas and sensations? Would he still be there if those were suddenly wiped out? No, he decided. "I think, therefore I am," was his famous conclusion. Descartes had reached rung 23, the discriminating intellect, but could not continue the climb to rung 25, the Inner Self. He was a philosopher; he lived for ideas and identified himself with his thoughts just as we identify with our jobs, our social roles, our emotions. Because Descartes was not a meditator in the yogic sense of the term, he did not sense the presence of a higher Self, an inner witnessing consciousness existing apart from the machinations of his mind. From the yogic point of view, he had merely practiced *pratyahara* (withdrawal of the senses from the external world and body) and *dharana* (contemplation), but had not yet reached the level of *nirvikalpa samadhi,* consciousness without an object. He therefore never noted a state in which his awareness rested in itself alone, without a material or subtle object to focus on.

According to the yoga texts there are a number of events which sometimes thrust people spontaneously into a vivid experience of the inner witnessing Self, the 25th *tattva.* One scripture states that while tasting a particularly delectable flavor, the soul may experience such enormous pleasure that it is instantly thrust back into its own perfect self nature. (I call this the Haagen Dazs sutra.) A more common way of involuntarily experiencing the *purusha* is to suddenly face deadly danger or unexpectedly receive extremely bad news. "I'm sorry to have to tell you this—I know this is sudden— but we just found your son by the side of the road. He's dead." The mind goes into shock. Thought stops. A tranquil but intensely vivid sense of one's own being occurs in that timeless moment. Most of us experience this extraordinary state only occasionally and generally only under extreme circumstances. Yogis deliberately cultivate this state of awareness, endeavoring to live and ultimately die in that state of tranquil observation.

Do you recognize this state? Even if you've never meditated in your life, odds are you've experienced the *purusha* several times at least. I remember a sudden patch of ice sending my Buick skidding off a winding mountain road. If you had told me a moment earlier that my car was about to spin out of control, plummet down a hill, twirl like a baton, take out a phone pole, and crumple like a tin can in a trash compactor while I sat helplessly in the driver's seat, I would probably have been terrified. But the experience was a pleasure. Once it registered that the car was out of control and that

Lalita

Durga

Sarasvati

Lakshmi

I was probably going to die, I was effortlessly drawn into the state of the inner witness, and sat perfectly relaxed behind the steering wheel watching the whole thing happen. Everything switched into slow motion. I remember in particular appreciating how beautiful the designs in the windshield appeared as it cracked into thousands of pieces. I even enjoyed being tossed to the passenger's side of the front seat while fractured glass spilled all over me (this was the last time in my life I drove without putting on my seat belt). I climbed out through the window when the car finally stopped (right after a toppling phone pole crushed the roof), totally calm and without a single scratch. Losing the car was a financial disaster but the state of consciousness I experienced during the accident was really interesting.

As we progress in meditation, we shift our awareness gradually inward through subtler states of matter until we leave the realm of matter completely and enter the heart of our own spirit. Each level along the way offers its peculiar, well-documented opportunities and pitfalls. For example, Patanjali mentions the *prakriti layas,* great masters whose field of consciousness has expanded to embrace *prakriti* itself meaning, incredible as this may sound, that their consciousness pervades the entire universe. But even this is not perfect liberation. According to Patanjali, liberation occurs only when all knowledge of the external universe is shut off.

The goal of classical yoga, as set forth in the *Yoga Sutras,* is "the establishment of the Self in the Self." The *Yoga Sutras* list numbers of *samadhis* or deep meditative states, most involving concentration on some material object, sensation or idea (in other words, any of categories 1-24). In the highest *samadhi,* called *nirvikalpa,* the Self cuts itself off from matter completely and rests in its own perfect, self-contained awareness. This is Patanjali's concept of liberation. There is one vast sea of matter, forming itself into various material and non-material elements. But there are an infinite number of Selves, and the goal of life is to return to one's own Self, completely turning away from the activities of nature and all the suffering and pain associated with them. Obviously this involves tremendous mental control and rigorous asceticism.

It's tempting to object, "Wait a minute! I don't experience myself as pure witnessing consciousness. I experience myself as a flesh and blood person with real thoughts and feelings. How can you say that this person inside me, the daily awareness which I experience as my very soul, isn't my true self?"

According to Patanjali, the inner witnessing consciousness never interacts with the first 24 cosmic evolutes. It is their *shaktis* or the innate energies of spirit and matter which interface, creating a field of ignorance called *asmita,* the mindfield which constitutes our ordinary awareness. Picture a magnet underneath a sheet of paper onto which iron shavings have been poured. The magnet and the iron never touch each other yet the *shakti* of the magnet interacts with the *shakti* of the iron so that the metal filings form a distinctive pattern on the paper. The field of energy between the pure, unsullied Self and unconscious matter is the soul. The soul—that is, you and I as we experience ourselves in our present unenlightened condition—is not actually real, say the yogis. The moon doesn't really shine; it is the sun's energy reflecting off its surface that gives the moon its light. You are pure consciousness reflecting through the vagaries of mind in hues such as happiness or depression. The ever unaffected consciousness within which witnesses these thoughts and moods, is the real you and never dies. That's the Self you're trying to make contact with in meditation.

This, incidently, is not just semantics: it was the actual experience of the yogis. The greatest mystics of the ancient Chinese tradition were called "immortals" because they established their moment-to-moment awareness in the undying center of consciousness beyond the mind. Everywhere in the world, yogis and Sufis, shamans and devotees, inner explorers of every culture and faith hang out in this perfectly undisturbed state of unalloyed consciousness called the Higher Self, an experience undiminished by the eventual death of the physical body.

It's not actually such a hard state to reach once you start paying attention to the mechanics of your internal awareness; even beginning meditators have glimpses of this level when they concentrate seriously. In fact, the purpose of yogic practices is not to help you achieve high states of consciousness—if you know what you're doing and apply a little will power, these higher states are fairly easily accessible. The real point of yoga *sadhana* is to help you remain in these high states once you reach them. The 20th century sage Ramana Maharshi, at the age of 17 and without any yogic training at all, achieved an enlightened state within a few minutes just by lying down on the floor and earnestly searching within for the answer to the ultimate question, "Who am I?" It took him years of absolutely one-pointed concentration, however, hiding in the basement of a temple at Arunachala, to become permanently established in that state. It's like learning to ride a bicycle. Many people experience high states of awareness which unfortunately come and go; they find their spiritual center, and then quickly teeter off. Few people are able to balance in a constant condition of perfect Self-awareness.

Classical yoga, like Buddhism, sees life as unremittingly painful, a condition to be escaped as rapidly as possible by establishing oneself in what Buddhists calls "the luminous clarity."This represents a withdrawal from life into transcendent being. Classical yoga is the set of mental and physical exercises described in the *Yoga Sutras* which sprang up to facilitate entry into and maintenance of "establishment in the Self."

UNCOVERING THE UNIVERSAL SELF

Because the degree of mental self-discipline necessary to achieve a sustained state of "establishment in the Self" seems so vast, I was horrified to hear Swami Rama Bharati refer to the *Yoga Sutras* as "a primer, a book for beginners."

"You mean," I thought desperately, "there's more?"

Indeed there is.

The great yogi and philosopher Adi Shankaracharya (believed by orthodox Hindus to have lived some time before Christ) was one of many sages who felt practitioners of classical yoga had stopped too soon in their inner exploration, offering an incomplete picture of the reality within. He himself experienced that his meditation took him not merely to the root of his own being, but to the heart of all being. He became convinced the Self he felt at his innermost core was ultimately the exact same Self everyone else also experiences. Many other mystics also reported that in high states of awareness, they experienced themselves not merely as one perfectly illumined soul, but as the conscious Self of all beings. They could find no limit to the reach of their awareness.

Accordingly, Shankaracharya taught that there are no individual Selves per se. *Atman,* the individual Self, is actually *Brahman,* the universal Self, he said. We are literally "all one." This perspective—called *advaita* or nondualistic Vedanta—is extremely ancient, but Shankaracharya wrote extensively about it and established monasteries throughout India propagating this doctrine, making it one of the most popular and influential philosophies in world history. It was called nondualistic because it acknowledged only one Spirit, a single underlying reality which never changes and beyond which nothing else could possibly exist.

But Shankaracharya faced a dilemma. In the deepest state of meditation he could reach, he experienced *satchidananda*—pure being, consciousness and bliss. But like the *purusha* of classical yoga, this supreme *Brahman* did not appear to do anything, it did not act. Therefore it could not have created the world. So how did the universe come into existence? It didn't, according to Shankaracharya—the universe we perceive is no more real than the snake we mistakenly believe we see when we stumble over a coiled rope in the dark. The universe is *maya,* a mysterious grand illusion, he concluded. *Prakriti* doesn't really exist. There is no such thing as matter, only Spirit exists.

Shankaracharya acknowledged that to individuals caught in the illusion, the world is definitely real, but he encouraged spiritual aspirants to look beyond the changing face of the material universe to the unchanging reality of divine awareness behind it. He advised his followers to renounce material life and spend their time contemplating the sacred verse, *Tat tvam asi,* "You are the immortal, all pervading Spirit, the Self of All."

TANTRA YOGA: ENLIGHTENMENT IN THE WORLD

While classical yoga was usually pursued by ascetics attempting to escape from the vicissitudes of life, and Vedanta was often practiced by monks who dismissed the world as ultimately an illusion, tantric practices were taken up by men and women living with their families, committed to making their lives in the material world happy and productive. Their dedication to fulfilling their social responsibilities and their respect for the natural world gave them a drastically different perspective than the renunciate yogis.

Like Shankaracharya, most major schools of Tantra are nondualistic: they hold that there is only one unitary reality. However, many tantric sects say that the Supreme Reality can be characterized not only by being, consciousness and bliss but also by will, knowledge and action. That is to say, the Supreme Universal Being is joyfully, willfully and wisely creative. In their deepest meditations, the tantrics experienced the Supreme Self as brimming with creative potency. (Can you tell we're edging up on the Goddess?)

Have you heard the old conundrum, "If God is all powerful, can he create a stone so big he can't lift it?" The tantric's answer is, "Definitely!" Infinite Being can and does impose finitehood upon itself, projecting both individual spirits and individual particles of matter from its own limitless being. According to the Shaktas, Shiva (here meaning all pervading Spirit, not the famous male deity) becomes *jiva*, the individual soul. Shiva also, by even further limiting his capacity to act and to know, becomes physical and subtle matter. This creative process is sometimes characterized as a primeval vibration or sound *(nada)* spreading from one central point of infinite potential *(bindu)* in waves of beauty and bliss. From this perspective the universe is the glory and majesty of God, projected from Divine Being. Matter is therefore no less inherently real or less sacred than spirit.

Thanks to Shiva's ability to make the infinite appear finite, most of us don't experience our Shivahood or being "one with God" at all. What distinguishes you from me, me from this book, and you, me and the book from Shiva, if our true nature is actually unlimited consciousness? Here come cosmic categories 26-30, the point in yogic cosmology where Tantra expands beyond the insights of classical yoga, which end with element 25, *purusha* or the individual Self. This Self is not the final reality, according to Shaktism, because individual souls experience five limiting conditions or constrictions of consciousness. These are:

26. The belief that we have finite boundaries and can therefore only get from here to there by traveling through space.
27. The belief that everything that happens now was caused by something which happened in the past (with the concomitant belief that we can therefore only move forward, not

backwards or sideways, in time).

28. The belief that we are incomplete and therefore need other things or other people in order to fulfill ourselves or make ourselves whole.
29. The belief that there is anything we don't know.
30. The belief that there is anything we can't accomplish.

Shiva, the Supreme Being, isn't subject to these constrictions. There is nothing he can't do, nothing he doesn't know, nothing apart from himself, and he's completely unbounded by time, space or causality. These five constrictions are caused by the 31st cosmic category, *maya. Maya* literally means "that which measures the unmeasurable." *Maya* sees limitation where none, in fact, exists. The cosmos is actually one unbounded mass of awareness/energy *(chit-shakti)*. The finite soul is unable to apprehend this unlimited unity all at once, because it identifies with a physical body, and permits itself to assimilate only the data supplied by its five senses. The five senses break the unlimited unitary reality down into cognizable chunks like you and me and this book.

There are three very subtle categories beyond *maya (tattvas* 32-34) through which we must pass before our Self can immerse itself in the Self of all. There's a state where matter appears more real than consciousness. Scientists reflect this perspective, considering human consciousness an epiphenomenon of the brain. There's another state where consciousness seems more real than matter. New Agers who claim we can control external reality merely by wishing hard enough represent this category. And there's a state where matter and consciousness seem equally real. None of these adequately describes reality. The truth, according to the tantrics, is that the entire universe and every living being in it is absolutely nothing but the supreme, self-existent consciousness/power itself, Shiva/Shakti *(tattvas* 36 and 35 respectively). Shiva/Shakti is that which simply is—before the beginning of the universe and eons after the universe ends—that which exists and knows it exists and creates the whole blissful universe at its pleasure.

There is one final *tattva,* the 37th category of being, sometimes called Maha Tripura Sundari or "the Supreme Beauty beyond the Triplicity" of the physical, subtle and causal dimensions. This is not actually a level of reality beyond Shiva and Shakti; rather it is meant to emphasize that Shiva and Shakti, pure being and the consciousness and power inherent in being, are not two separate entities but one unitary reality. And Maha Tripura Sundari is Lalita, the Goddess, the player whose game this whole kit and caboodle is. We've stepped off the top of the ladder of the universe and find ourselves ensconced in the lap of the Mother of the Universe.

What are the repercussions of this worldview for spiritual practitioners? Imagine you're a yogi or yogini who's spent years in intensive meditation, and you've discovered the Higher Self within yourself, a realm of absolute tranquility undisturbed by thoughts and sensations. Advanced practitioners can sit unmoving in this state for weeks on end, their metabolism slowed to the point that normal body functions, such as the need to eat or drink or excrete, disappear. Yogic lore speaks of adepts sitting absolutely still for such long periods that ant hills grew up around them. Even in modern times cases of yogis voluntarily buried alive, surviving for days under the earth, barely breathing, have been authenticated. These adepts are not unconscious; on the contrary they are in a state of intense lucidity, but no *vrittis* or thought waves are disrupting their total absorption in the state of pure Self-consciousness. Classical yogis have now only to wait for death when pure consciousness is released from any association with a physical body whatever, and liberation is attained.

Tantrics, however, are not looking for liberation *from* the world but for enlightenment *in* the world. In a Shakta classic called the *Tripura Rahasya,* a prince named Hemachuda achieved the state of establishment of the Self in the Self, the goal of classical yoga. He sat in deep meditative absorption day after day, not wanting to be disturbed. Finally his wife, an advanced tantric adept, interrupted his *sadhana,* teasing, "My darling, you are as far from enlightenment as a reflection of the stars in a pond is from the sky! What kind of liberation is this that dissolves when you open your eyes?" She went on to explain that the true goal of yoga is *sahaja samadhi,* maintaining awareness of the divine reality while fulfilling one's responsibilities in the world.

From the tantric perspective, the cosmos is not something "other" from which we need to escape. It, like us, was projected by the divine feminine force (*tattva* 35) from the pure being of the divine masculine principle (*tattva* 36) at the beginning of creation. Therefore it is completely holy and worthy of our highest veneration. Enlightenment means not only recognizing that "I am Shiva—pure consciousness" but recognizing that everything else in the universe is also Shiva. It means embracing all of reality with eyes wide open and arms open wide. In a heart brimming with love, there is no room for fear.

The 37th level of reality—Lalita—is the end of the line, the deepest experience any yogi has ever had. Yet one of the Supreme Goddess's powers is unconditional free will. Those of us who are conscious sparks of her all consuming fire share in her free will. Because of this, we can look up and say, "I'm not part of the Goddess! I'm me! I'll do things my own way!" And because the Goddess is full of bliss, she'll look at that tiny point of individuated consciousness with total delight and smile, "Go for it!" The Mother of the Universe will give the ego everything it wants, and then take it all away, until the soul gets disgusted with being born and dying, with gaining and losing, and cries that it wants to come home.

THE WAY HOME

I have a computer which allows me to click on any of a number of icons (colorful images appearing on my computer screen) in order to access the wealth of information stored in my hard drive. The Hindu perspective is, "Go ahead and click any icon which works for you. Any one of them will connect you with the hard drive. In fact, if you don't see an icon you like, go ahead and create your own." The orthodox Christian perspective is, "No, don't do that! The Jesus icon is the only one which will take you to the hard drive. All the others are false icons." The Muslim view is, "Under no circumstances are you to use any icons whatsoever. They will lead you to confuse the reality of the hard drive with the ridiculous little images on the computer screen." Islam is, in effect, the MS-DOS of world religions.

It's human nature to believe one's own conception of the Supreme Being is the correct icon, or at least the best one. Even the great sages of Hinduism occasionally feud with each other over exactly how to view the Supreme Being, over whose path to that divine reality is superior, and whose level of enlightenment is "highest." The *Tripura Rahasya* tells of one such argument which broke out when some of the greatest Vedic seers—including no less illustrious figures than Vasishtha, Vishvamitra, Kasyapa, Bhrigu, Parashara, and Narada—gathered in Satya Loka (a subtle level of existence far beyond the physical plane) for a discussion. Each became exasperated that the others didn't share his views. Finally they all tramped off to the great God Brahma to settle their dispute.

"Lord Brahma, you are the Creator of the universe and the grandfather of us all. We are all considered to be enlightened sages, yet the forms of spiritual practice we embrace differ from one of us to the next. Some of us are wholly devoted to serving all sentient beings, while others of us prefer to remain at home, singing the praise of the divine, pouring out our love for the Supreme Being. Still others sit absorbed in profound states of meditation, without a single thought disturbing the vast expanse of their tranquil awareness. Which of us has found the highest way?"

Brahma looked out over the shining mindfields of the sages and realized that no matter which answer he gave, he was sure to get into trouble. "You know, that's a really tough question," he blustered. "Let's go ask Lord Shiva. He'll definitely know!"

But Shiva (here signifying once again the male deity) also recognized the quagmire offering his opinion would get him into. No matter which sage he hailed as the greatest, the others would disagree, feeling their philosophical systems and methods of spiritual practice made them superior. There was only one thing to do. "I'm not completely sure what to say. So let's all meditate on Maha Tripura Sundari, the source of all knowledge, radiant consciousness Lalita herself. Through her grace, we may find the answer."

Together Brahma, Shiva, and all the sages focused their awareness on the feet of the Mother of the Universe. Rumbling like thunder, the voice of the Divine Mother shook the sky of their minds. "My darling children, tell me what you require. I always fulfill the desires of my devotees."

Prostrate with awe, Brahma cried out, "Mother of all, pure bliss itself, we bow before you again and again. You are the self existent reality, ever fresh as a 16-year-old girl because, since you are beginningless and endless, you never age or decay. You are the ever flowing font of blessings which gives birth to the worlds, nourishes them and takes them away. You are the supreme happiness every living thing seeks consciously or unconsciously. Over and over and over again, we bow in loving adoration.

"Mother, you already know the question we have brought before you. Please be gracious and remove our confusion."

Smiling at the quarreling sages, Lalita lovingly revealed the nature of the universe and the true value of spiritual discipline. "The entire universe, which appears so real to entities of finite intelligence, in fact is no more inherently real than a reflection in a mirror," she began. "My devotees, cleansing the mirror of their awareness with tranquility, concentration and loving devotion, discover me at the root of all things, self-luminous, transparent, and perfect.

"Beyond the grip of the material worlds lies an island made of priceless gems, resting on a sea of bliss. In the center of that island is a temple of light, where I sit on my throne of limitless dimensions made of numberless universes both material and immaterial. Draw your awareness up your spine into my antechamber, and I will admit you into my throne room.

"All the entities in all the worlds, from the highest gods to the humblest, barely conscious creatures, are fragments of my glory. Throughout myriad world systems I am worshipped by all beings, though they call me by different names. I reward them according to the intensity of their worship. How many beings—a number beyond your ability to conceive—are worshiping me at this very moment, and yet how few of them actually know me!

"The creatures I have created imagine they exist apart from me, but this is no more real than a kingdom one travels through in a dream. The realization that they are in fact integral parts of the unity of my being comes to them only through deep, sustained devotion to me. When the mind with all its thoughts and feelings is directed solely towards me, the soul discovers its unity with me. The realization that only one unlimited consciousness exists anywhere and everywhere is liberating knowledge. When obstructions limiting the individual soul fall away, the Self recognizes it is not limited to its body, and has never been and will never be anything other than my own Self. When this experience occurs, all doubts vanish like clouds chased away by a strong wind. One who has merged in me exists beyond all suffering and does not know fear.

"Souls are afraid because they imagine something exists outside themselves that can threaten them. When they recognize that nothing exists beyond their own inherent divine nature, there is nothing left to fear. Where can darkness hide when the Sun rises?

"Most souls are not aware of their true identity. From the perfect wisdom innate within me, I send pure hearted saints and inspiring scriptures to remind them who they are. When a soul remembers its union with me, it continues to fulfill its duties in the external world which still plays before its senses, but inwardly it remains aware of the interconnectedness of all things, even while in the dream and deep sleep states.

"In order to reach this level of enlightenment, unwavering determination is essential. Depending on one's degree of purity and commitment, one can find me in a matter of days, months, years, or lifetimes. There are three major obstacles which undermine the seeker's efforts. Lack of firm faith in my existence or in his or her own capacity to reach me is the first. Doubts nag at the mind, sapping one's energy and enthusiasm. Keeping the company of saints, studying the scriptures, and carefully discriminating between the aspects of my nature which pass away and those which are eternal, lead one beyond doubt.

"The second problem is preoccupation with sexuality, other forms of sensual pleasure, and personal goals. The aspirant is continually distracted because he or she delights in the world; why seek anything beyond it? Nonattachment must be cultivated, for one can never embrace the eternal with arms still wrapped around objects of the world. These objects turn to dust and blow away even as one clings to them.

"The third problem is laziness. Many seekers know that life is short, that death will arrive all too soon, and sincerely aspire to find that which is immortal, yet old habits prevent them from devoting themselves to the quest in earnest. But it isn't possible to uncover the undying reality behind one's mental states without intensive spiritual practice. The remedy for spiritual inertia, which motivates one to persevere enthusiastically, is loving devotion to me. Loving me leads to desire for union with me; recognizing the ceaseless flow of my grace in one's life opens one's eyes and leads one to see me everywhere, in everything.

"Whatever the religion, whatever the form of spiritual practice, the truth is that all spiritually motivated efforts have only one goal: to attain me. I myself inspire my devotees to make the supreme effort required to find me. One who endeavors to practice spirituality without all consuming love for me is like a blind person stumbling in the dark. Love for me illuminates the heart and sweetens the bitter taste of the self-discipline required.

"The aspirant who is absolutely committed to spiritual practice is truly great. The one whose heart is also brimming with love is even greater. The one whose awareness remains continually centered in my consciousness, being and bliss, is the greatest of all.

"Some aspirants are distracted by the desire for psychic powers. None of these powers carries one beyond time and space into the heart of my being. All the supernatural powers put together are not worth a fraction of the value of true Self-realization. Why waste one's time developing powers which inflame one's egotism and are directed at acquiring things which are continually passing away? My devotees do not pursue psychic powers, but psychic powers pursue them. When their hearts and minds remain centered on me, miracles occur around them continually, without their having to pause one moment to will such things to happen. All true miracles come from me, the center of perfect well-being within yourselves.

"There are three levels of Self-realization. The first is that which endures as long as one sits quietly in meditation. The second is that which lasts throughout the day, provided one does not have to specifically concentrate on some external activity. But the greatest state of Self-realization is that which never wavers, whether in the waking, dream or sleep states, whether meditating, relaxing, or working hard, that which is completely effortless, which has become the natural, spontaneous state of my devotee. Remaining easily in this state, one is joyful, loving, non-clinging, undisturbed, free from doubt and full of knowledge. Being completely fulfilled, my devotee remains contentedly desireless. The one who is absolutely fearless and pure, who sees all other beings, the wise and the foolish, the good and evil, as parts of his or her own unlimited being, I call that sage the highest. Such a one is completely established in me and I am completely established in him or her. Between this perfected one's awareness and my own, you will find no difference whatsoever.

"I have answered your question. Now surrender your attachment to your own views and rest your consciousness in mine. We have never been and will never be apart. I am in you and you are in me. This is the reality."

Having spoken this *Vidya Gita* (Song of Knowledge), Lalita smiled and disappeared. The seers, beaming with increased richness of understanding, joyfully headed home, their confusion dispelled and their egotism defused. The *Vidya Gita* concludes by promising that the Divine Mother's advice is a boat which can carry all of us across the ocean of suffering, and an unfailing light to those lost in the dark.

THE TEN SECRET GODDESSES

There are ten major goddesses in the esoteric yogic tradition. Of these, the three most widely worshiped are the fierce and mighty Kali, the ever-wise Tara, and lovely, gracious Lalita.

While Sarasvati, Lakshmi, Kali and Durga are enormously popular goddesses whose images can be found from one end of India to the other, Lalita is an esoteric goddess, worshiped quietly by the Shakta yogis, by monks in Hindu monasteries such as those established by Shankaracharya, and by lay initiates privately in their homes. The simplest villagers can relate to the popular goddesses and the boons they grant, but Lalita is a more abstract deity, the living power of absolute consciousness, and the boon she confers, Self-realization, is less in demand than success in school, rupees, or healing from a disease.

Lalita nevertheless is anthropomorphized by the tradition as a voluptuous young woman carrying five arrows made of long-stemmed flowers, a bow made of sugar cane, a noose and a goad. The arrows are our five senses and the bow with which they're dispatched is our mind. When our senses are offered to the Goddess and our thoughts are directed to the divine, our lives become sweet and fragrant. But when we find ourselves pausing on the spiritual path, taking time to indulge ourselves in one distraction or another, Lalita gently prods us along with her goad. If we resist her gentle suggestion that it's time to move along, to come back into the house after playing outside, she lassoes us with her noose and drags us, kicking and screaming, back to her lap. Many of us have experienced this lasso. It's often quite painful but it's also the fullest expression of Lalita's love.

Kala is the Sanskrit word for time; Kali is the empress of the time force. She removes everything from us that is less than divine, purifying us in searing flames of inevitable loss. She is, as one yogi expressed, "the terrible mother who lashes mortal man with the scourge of death, to drive us towards immortality." Tantra yoga is a path of fire and light; on this path the fire comes first. Kali takes away the people and things we love in order to leave us, at the end of our harrowing journey, with love alone. The esoteric Kali is not as sentimentalized as the more popular version of Kali. In the esoteric tradition one is called to face the full horror of the devastating indifference of nature's forces and of the bottomless depravity of human nature. This Kali is not consoling, but for anyone who's watched a loved one die or been forced to face their own mortality, she is inescapably real. There is no way to avoid her; we will all feel the blade of her sword cutting through the veins in our neck soon enough. Every sentient being in the cosmos, including the highest gods, are destined to become bloody sacrifices on the altar of time. It takes courage to love and accept Kali. Her boon to those who worship her sincerely is absolute fearlessness.

Tara, the Goddess who carries us safely across the churning ocean of transmigration, has long been a beloved protectress of the Buddhists. However, her tradition can be traced back to extremely ancient times in North India. In the *Yajur Veda,* one of the earliest surviving scriptures of humanity, the seer sings, "Let us rise to the Universal Mother, who is a swift and unsinking ship, spacious as the earth itself, who carries us safely to the furthest shore." Beautiful paintings of Tara are commonly met in Bengal, where the compassionate Goddess is frequently depicted guiding young children safely over treacherous waters. If Kali represents the stormy sea of time in which the boats of our lives must ultimately sink, and Lalita represents the safe harbor, Tara is the force which ensures that we reach the mystical gem island in the thousand-petaled *chakra* at the roof of the brain, that part of us which lies outside of time and space, undying.

If Kali is divine consciousness in the indomitable form of time, Bhuvaneshvari (Empress of All Planes of Existence) is the Goddess as infinite, trackless space. She contains everything; all world systems evolve within her formless, limitless body. Westerners tend to think of space as simple void or emptiness. To the yogis however, every cubic nanometer of space is permeated with divine awareness. In fact, without the will of the Divine Mother, it would be impossible for space to exist or be perceived. It is through the will of the infinitely extensive, omnipresent Goddess Bhuvaneshvari that matter and energy begin their play, and consciousness takes a shape, as if it were delimited within the theater of space.

Bhairavi, like Kali, is a warrior Goddess. Just as Lalita is called Tripura Sundari, "The Supreme Beauty in the Three Planes of Existence," Bhairavi is called Tripura Bhairavi, "The Supreme Terror in the Three Worlds." She is *chid agni,* the fire of consciousness which incinerates every impurity. Yogis honor her with intense programs of personal austerity. She is said to blaze up the subtle channels in the spine, burning away every obstruction between our root humanity, seated at the base of the spine in yogic physiology, and the inherent divinity enthroned at the top of our skulls.

The goddesses of the yogic lineages are all utterly extraordinary. Bagala, for example, is the deity who stops thought. She is so stunningly beautiful that the faintest glimpse of her shocks the mind into silence while the pure beauty within unobstructedly irradiates the field of our awareness. Dhumavati, on the other hand, is anthropomorphized as withered and ugly, old and withdrawn. Her thin breasts are dry and drooping, representing her unwillingness to nurture. She is one of the very rare appearances in the Hindu tradition of the Goddess as widow. Philosophically she represents the condition of the universe at the end of its multi-billion year cycle of manifestation, when matter and energy slip into abeyance and the universal life force withdraws itself. She is the Supreme Silence, deeper than death, the remotest and most intangible mystery. Only the very greatest of yogis can maintain full consciousness in her presence.

Matangi is young and beautiful, a gifted artist and speaker, but she has compromised her virtue. She is the power of self-expression, and the yogi engaged in her *sadhana* worships her through dance or painting or singing. She is metaphorically considered "compromised" because the Supreme Goddess's greatest powers exist deep within consciousness. At the articulated level—our physical plane of existence—her powers are diluted. The material universe, awesome as it is, has the capacity to express only the tiniest fraction of a fraction of her majesty.

Kamala, young, beautiful and victorious, embodies another view of the physical world. Kamala means lotus, and this deity represents the full flowering of the Supreme Goddess in the form of the worlds. She is wholly benevolent and radiates blessings, spiritual and material, in every moment. As one of the ten great goddesses of the yoga tradition, she signals that those who wholeheartedly adore the Goddess receive from her not only enlightenment but pleasure, luxury and all auspicious comforts. The difference between an ordinary hedonist and a worshiper of Kamala is that her devotee understands that all the wonderful things we enjoy in life belong to the Goddess, not to us, and therefore he or she is happy to release these things when the Mother of the Universe wants them back.

Chinnamasta is perhaps the single most shocking deity in the entire Hindu pantheon. She has severed her own head, which she holds in one of her hands. Three streams of blood shoot from her gaping neck. Female servants drink from two of the streams; her own decapitated head swallows the third. The mystical significance of Chinnamasta's gruesome sacrifice is readily apparent. The Divine Mother loves her children so much, even the worst of them, that she offers her own blood to nourish them. Chinnamasta is the most explicit illustration of the apparently ghastly self-replenishing forces of nature I've ever seen. Life feeds on life to sustain itself. Serving herself to her children, the Mother of the Universe is fed herself.

I've been told by a North Indian yogi that Chinnamasta's is one of the fastest paths to enlightenment, but it requires its practitioner to literally die. The fulfillment of the practice comes only after having deliberately vacated one body and entered another in full consciousness. More details than that, I don't know.

Yet of the esoteric Goddess lineages, Kali and Lalita's are

preeminent. Lalita is worshipped on the full moon because its waxing phases represent the increasing light of the soul as it expands to joyously embrace the entire universe. Lalita grants every desire from the hunger for sex to the yearning for the liberating knowledge of cosmic consciousness. Lalita is young, gloriously beautiful, costumed in light. Kali, however, is worshipped during the new moon because its waning phases show the soul letting go of its attachment to all phenomena, all belongings, all thought. Kali extinguishes desire, replacing it with the liberating knowledge of mystical experience. Kali is ancient, emaciated, naked, enrobed in darkness. Lalita is *purna*, everything, fullness; Kali is *sunyata*, nothing, the void. The Shakta scriptures emphasize again and again that just as there is only one Moon, whether it is new or full, waxing or waning, Kali and Lalita are the same Goddess, and their paths are not two but one.

Lalita is an exquisitely sensuous Goddess also known as Kameshvari (Empress of Desire), self-willed and independent. At the same time, she is the completely devoted consort of the Supreme Lord Shiva. She exists in a perpetual state of perfect harmony, though from time to time she takes up arms, for the gross and violent forces of evil can overwhelm the worlds unless she intervenes to restore balance.

The *Tripura Rahasya* says, "That which shines within as pure being is Her Majesty, the Supreme Empress, Absolute Consciousness. The universe and all the creatures that range within it are that One Reality. Yes, all this is She alone."

In the following excerpt from the same text, the Goddess of Supreme Beauty further explains who she is—and who we are.

Tripura Rahasya:
THE MYSTERY OF THE TRIUNE GODDESS

The Goddess speaks:

> I am the intelligence from which the universe emanates
>   and in which it abides.
> The ignorant believe that I am merely nature
>   but the wise experience me as the true Self within
>   themselves.

They glimpse me in their own hearts
    when their minds become as still and clear as an ocean
    without waves.

All gods and all creatures in all planes of existence
    are manifestations of myself.
My power is too vast to be imagined.
You do not know me because your mind is shrouded by
    ignorance.
That too is my power.

The supreme wisdom is that which ends the delusion
    that anything exists apart from myself.
The fruit of this realization is fearlessness
    and the end of sorrow.
When one realizes that all the limitless universes
    are a fraction of an atom in the unity of my being,
    that all the numberless lives in the universes
    are a wisp of vapor in one of my breaths,
    that all triumphs and tragedies, the good and evil
    in all the worlds,
    are merely games I play for my own amusement,
    then life and death stand still,
    and the drama of individual life evaporates
    like a shallow pond on a warm day.

You are experiencing me now
    yet you do not recognize me.
There is no remedy for your ignorance other than to worship
    me as your innermost Self.
Surrender your self to me with joyful, one-pointed devotion,
    and I will help you discover your true being.
Abide in the core of your being—you will find me there.
Abide in me as I abide in you.
Know that even now, in this very moment,
    there is absolutely no difference between us.
Realize it this instant!

6

Kundalini: The Goddess as the
Illuminating Energy of Awareness

WHO ARE YOU?

One of my most favorite stories from the *Vedas* occurs in the
Kena Upanishad. The demi-gods are partying, slapping each other
on the back, congratulating themselves for having just won a major
battle against the demons. Suddenly in the distance they notice a
stranger, glowing peculiarly. "Who is that?" they wonder. Agni is
dispatched to find out.

The brazen demi-god struts up to the newcomer and loudly
demands, "Who are you?"

"Who are *you?*" the shining being quietly responds.

"I am Agni, fire!" the warrior proudly exclaims. "I am the fire in
the sacrificial pit, I am the fire that shines as the sun in the sky, and
at the death of the universe I burn away all the worlds! I am the
greatest force in the cosmos! I can burn anything!"

"Burn this." The stranger holds up a tiny piece of straw.

Insulted at the trifling challenge, Agni decides to teach the
mysterious visitor a lesson. Summoning all the power at his command, he furiously attacks the dry blade of grass.

Nothing happens. The straw is not even singed.

"Well, it's been nice meeting you," the fire god stammers. "I, uh,
have another appointment. If you'll excuse me. . . ." Agni beats a
hasty retreat.

"So who was that?" the other demi-gods ask.

"How should I know?" Agni retorts angrily. "Go find out for
yourselves!"

Next Vayu heads over to confront the luminous stranger. "Who
are you?" he shouts.

"Who are *you?*" the stranger echoes softly.

"I am Vayu, wind! I blow away entire villages! I can blow the sea into a swirling current in the sky! At the death of the universe I blow away the ashes of the worlds!"

"Blow this." The stranger holds up the piece of straw.

Infuriated, Vayu throws himself at the straw with all his might. It doesn't even quiver.

"Well, I gotta go. You take care now!" Vayu quickly vanishes, huffing with embarrassment.

This is getting irritating. The demi-gods decide to send Indra, their chieftain and the greatest of all warriors in heaven, to uncover the truth. But by the time Indra arrives the glowing being has disappeared. Indra searches and searches until finally he spots a minute golden glow far in the distance. Gradually it comes closer, becoming more dazzling the nearer it approaches. Squinting against the blazing light, Indra makes out the form of a stunningly beautiful woman named Uma, of bright gold complexion, wearing a sparkling golden sari.

"Excuse me!" Indra calls. "There was a stranger standing here a little while ago. Can you tell me who he was?"

Uma's eyes flash. "That was the all pervading reality," she replies. And the story abruptly ends.

I remember one of my college professors, a Jesuit scholar of some stature, mocking this story one day in class. Four thousand years ago, the superstitious Indo-European priests of India would gather around campfires at night and entertain each other with silly and meaningless tales like this one about their ludicrous pagan deities, my professor claimed.

"Isn't it odd," I ventured, "if this is such a silly and meaningless story, that the brahmin priests preserved it in their oral tradition for many thousands of years, never allowing succeeding generations to alter even one syllable?"

"The Hindus retain many unintelligible stories in their scriptures," he answered curtly.

I sat there with my mouth hanging open. The grandeur of the parable was so obvious I could hardly believe Western scholars could miss it—most meditators would recognize its spiritual significance immediately. The demi-gods falsely believed they had won a victory. In fact it is the eternally luminous inner awareness, the Supreme One, the source of life, energy, will and desire, which makes any victory possible. The Sanskrit word for demi-god is *devata*, which also signifies the senses. The text is saying that we identify with our senses imagining that we—the body, the personality—act in the world of our own accord. In fact it is divine awareness, perfect consciousness beyond the reach of the senses, which fire cannot burn, which the wind cannot blow away, which gives us the ability to breathe, to perceive, to create, to win.

Indra is king of the demi-gods, that is, lord of the senses. He is the masterful soul, the yogi who withdraws his awareness from his external senses and searches within for the answer to the eternal question, "Who are you?" The Goddess Uma, the force the yogis call *kundalini,* the power of enlightenment, flashes within and in her revelatory light Indra discovers his own true nature: all pervading being pulsing with self-awareness, creative power, and bliss. Agni and Vayu didn't grasp that when they asked God, "Who are you?" and he responded, "Who are *you?*" he was answering their question. If they had looked within themselves for the mysterious source of light they had sensed but couldn't understand, they would have found in their own hearts the one they were seeking. God's true identity is revealed only when we discover who *we* are.

Like Agni and Vayu, most of us don't understand what the divine light really is, though now and then we catch glimpses of its dazzling luminosity, in moments of great joy for example, or at the time of near-death experiences when we may see it burning intensely at the end of a long, dark tunnel. The spiritual quest requires us, as it required Indra, to seek within ourselves for our true identity because when we discover our deepest, highest Self, we have uncovered God. "Superstitious" Hindus "sitting around their campfires four thousand years ago" understood this. Modern scholars sitting in front of their computer screens don't have a clue.

Years later in graduate school I watched as a swami visiting from India tried to explain these truths to a Western audience, struggling to express himself in today's universal language—broken English. Groping for words, he painstakingly explained that within every living being is a conscious center of perfect awareness whose circumference extends beyond the furthest reaches of the cosmos.

"Look within," he emphasized in thickly accented English. "You must look inside yourselves."

One of the women in the classroom interrupted timidly. "What if we look within, and we don't like what we see?"

I'll never forget the expression on the swami's face. He was completely dumbfounded. He hadn't been in America long enough to learn that our spiritual teachers have taught us that we're depraved—abhorrent sinners in the eyes of God. Secular religions like psychoanalysis and its modern popular offspring take up the chorus: we are perpetual victims of parental abuse, our ids seethe with taboo sexual and aggressive impulses, our lives are scarred with unmanageable neuroses. When we were children our culture certainly never hinted that if we looked into the deepest recesses of our being, we would find God. So instead we look into ourselves and see hatred, lust and fear.

The tantric tradition calls these negativities *kleshas,* mental afflictions, or sometimes more graphically *asuras,* demons. We can wrestle with our inner demons as long as we want or need to, and believe me the tantric system provides some pretty colorful methods for doing just that, but eventually a day dawns when we get really sick of fighting with ourselves. Then the *guru shakti,* the enlightening power of the universe, can begin to act in us. We start contemplating a higher reality, perhaps even meditating, and discover that buried deep beneath the muck of the sub-conscious lies the clarity and healing power of the super-conscious. The *Tripura Rahasya* compares this Higher Self to a priceless gem locked in a chest that's buried in mud. Spiritual discipline consists of cleaning away the mud of our petty desires and resentments, then prying open the treasure box of our brain and its subtle centers to unlock the incalculable wealth of Self-awareness and divine power within.

In my early teens I had a dream so vivid I remember it in detail. I was in a stagecoach galloping westward during the Gold Rush. Like my fellow passengers, I was flush with excitement at the prospect of how wealthy I was about to become. As the coach pulled up in California, we all leapt out without bothering to collect our luggage, grabbed shovels, and ran out into the fields to begin shoveling gold into our gunny sacks. All around us, a foot deep, was cow dung. Delirious with greed, we were shoveling manure into our bags as fast as we could heave it! My heart was actually racing with excitement and exertion. An old man, the only calm person in my dream, walked up, stood beside me quietly for a moment, and finally offered, "That isn't gold. It's shit!"

I was irritated at being interrupted; time was money. Suddenly I noticed some of the dung had splattered on my pants and, with a horrible shock, I realized the old man was right! Staring with repulsion at my filthy, stinking pants, I remembered a prayer from the Lutheran liturgy, "Remove from me the soiled garment of my sin."

The dream startled me awake. I turned over and went back to sleep. This time I found myself on a starship in the vastness of outer space. Around me were computer databases filled with records of innumerable galaxies, exobiotic life forms and extraterrestrial cultures. Trembling with excitement, I tried to operate one of the consoles but the monitor readouts responded with complex geometric patterns I couldn't understand. It was maddeningly frustrating to have universal knowledge at my fingertips, and not be able to access it! The old man from my previous dream reappeared beside me. "You're not prepared," he said. "Study and meditate, and you will know."

The beginning of spiritual life is like being trapped in an elevator stuck between floors. We no longer mistake cow manure for treasure but the rewards of spiritual knowledge still lie beyond our grasp. We're no longer wholly engrossed in gossiping with friends, watching TV, or carefully monitoring our financial portfolios, because we've sensed something higher. But still we can't completely let go of our ordinary preoccupations either, in order to rise to the next floor. And since the two levels of reality, material and spiritual, seem so radically different, we can't even begin to imagine how to integrate the two.

In the often long and lonely search for who we really are, we may give up and turn back like Agni and Vayu. Only those who persevere, like Indra, are blessed with the grace of the Goddess Uma. When we propitiate her with faith, humility and determination, the Goddess of Revelation streaks up the subtle channel in our spine, explodes into our brain, and illumines our inner truth. In the yoga tradition Uma is known as Brahma Vidya, "Knowledge of the Supreme Reality." Today we call her *kundalini.*

THE ASHES OF LOVE

How does *kundalini* operate? For a few hints, let's turn to the *Brahmanda Purana*, a thousand year old text from South India, where the following story (forty chapters long in the original version—I've abridged substantially!) appears.

Lord Shiva was engaged in ascetic practices, sitting absorbed in deep meditation, when he suddenly felt a flush of lust. Though two of his eyes remained shut in contemplation, his third eye flickered open, looking for the force which had disturbed his concentration. Sure enough, there was Kama, the God of Love, grinning wickedly, having just unleashed an arrow of desire at Shiva, Lord of the Yogis. Instantly a laser-like bolt arced from Shiva's open eye, incinerating Kama. That annoying distraction removed, the eyelid fluttered shut and the Lord resumed his interrupted meditation.

From the ashes of love arose the demon Bhanda, flaming with desire for power, wealth and sensual indulgence. Seeing the Lord of the Universe seated in meditation before him, Bhanda propitiated Shiva with such fierce intensity that Shiva granted him a boon: that whenever Bhanda made war on an enemy, half his enemy's power would be transferred directly to Bhanda.

Bhanda quickly became a mighty king, conquering a vast dominion and ruling a large, resplendent court. He was dominated by lust, however, and from time to time would completely lose interest in his conquests and spend years on end frittering away the time in the company of beautiful women.

During one of these interludes the sage Narada appeared to Indra and the other demi-gods to warn them of the increasing threat Bhanda represented. "His devotion to Lord Shiva has made Bhanda incalculably strong, both in terms of physical might and psychic powers. Don't ignore his growing power or disaster is sure to come. You must worship Mother Para Shakti, the Supreme Energy, and she will help you ward off this menace."

Thoroughly alarmed, Indra made his way to the Himalayas to perform penances in order to gain the inner strength necessary to defeat Bhanda. On the bank of the Bhagirathi river, "blooming profusely with every kind of splendid flower," Indra worshiped the Mother of the Universe. The setting where he performed this practice is called Indra Prastha, because all who do spiritual practice there attain their desires.

The planet Venus noticed what Indra was up to and rushed to Bhanda's court—where all venusian pleasures were joyfully entertained—to alert the demons. Quickly assembling an army, Bhanda hurried to Indra Prastha to disrupt Indra's penance. Seeing the demons coming to disturb her divine son's meditation, the Mother of the Universe instantly threw up a protective wall. With considerable effort, the demons smashed the wall but the very moment it crumbled, another bulwark appeared in its place. The demon army tried again, and again, but defensive walls continued to materialize out of the ether.

Meanwhile Indra called the rest of the demi-gods together and announced, "Bhanda's army is so powerful, there is no way we can defeat him on our own. We will have to dig a fire pit a mile long and propitiate the Goddess with the *mahamansa yagna*— human sacrifice." So they lit a great fire and offered human hands and feet, head and torso, blood and internal organs, as they chanted the mantras sacred to the Mother of the Universe.

A circular mass of blazing light materialized over the fire. At the center of the shining wheel sat the Great Goddess, resplendent as the rising sun. The demi-gods recognized her immediately: she was the life force of the entire cosmos, the quintessence of beauty and desire, adorned in robes the color of pomegranate, smiling at them with a loving glance as cool as moonlight. In her four arms she held a noose, a goad, a sugarcane bow and five arrows tipped with flower petals. She was manifesting as Lalita, the embodiment of Self-awareness.

What is the text saying? To those initiated in the Shakta tradition, the meaning is instantly clear. It is not possible to annihilate the force of desire within ourselves, because this force arises from Kameshvari, the Empress of Desire who is none other than the Mother of the Universe herself. Attempting to suppress his desires, Shiva tried to obliterate the demi-god Kama, Lord of Sexual Desire, but another powerful entity instantly took Kama's place. Unlike Kama, who represents the sacred movement of nature to cherish others and reproduce itself, Bhanda represented distorted, aggressive, selfish lust.

Indra, the masterful soul, resorts to the Himalayas to do spiritual practices which will restore a healthy, God-centered lifestyle. In yogic literature an immovable mountain represents the spinal column, which remains upright and unwavering in meditation. The Bhagirathi river on the banks of which Indra does penance is the *sushumna*, the subtle nerve current which is the conduit for *kundalini*, beginning at the base of the spine and emptying into the brain. Indra Prastha, the "flower-strewn" city where Indra meditates, is the *sahasrara chakra*, the thousand petalled lotus at the top of the brain. Holding his consciousness in this highest *chakra*, Indra enters *nirvikalpa samadhi*, the deepest state of meditation, where he becomes impregnable. The Divine Mother Uma protects him from the onslaught of the demons—his own anti-divine impulses—so long as he remains in this fortress, a yogic state beyond thought and desire.

But it is not Indra's destiny to sit withdrawn in meditation for the rest of his life. His *dharma* or life purpose is to rule the demigods, that is to rule his senses and inner spiritual powers so that he can act successfully and beneficently in the world. So he mentally summons all his internal energies to make the supreme sacrifice, the one form of human sacrifice which is genuinely spiritually effective: offering every cell of one's own body into the fire pit of *kundalini*. Having purified himself physically, emotionally and mentally, Indra becomes fit for the vision of the Mother of the Universe, the Supreme Power of consciousness herself. She—the source of universal consciousness—is seated in a luminous orb just above the thousand petalled *chakra* at the top of the head.

At the sight of Para Shakti, the power of consciousness, the soul and its inner senses are subsumed in rapture. Indra and the demigods cry out:

Victory to the Mother of the Universe,
     greater than the greatest,
     source of prosperity and well being,
     the holiness of the act of love!
Victory to the inexpressible beauty of consciousness,
     the protectress of the three worlds,
     pervading unlimited space
     yet fully manifest in every atom!

It is you who, in an act of overflowing love,
 give birth to all beings.
The dawn is your robe,
 the past, present and future are your body,
 and the scriptures are your words.
You reside in the hearts of the pure-minded,
 where you sit invisibly
 bestowing wealth, happiness and love.
You hold up the earth in empty space;
 the sun arises in you.
We bow again and again to the incomprehensible Goddess
 who creates, sustains and withdraws the galaxies.
You are the primordial guru, ever filled
 with wisdom and delight.
Your power has no beginning, middle or end—
 the magnificence of your being is beyond description!

Smiling at the upturned faces of the enraptured demi-gods, which glowed with the reflection of her own light, the Goddess Lalita said, "My dear ones, be joyous! I will remove your fear. I bless all of you with virtue, prosperity and fame, and with loving spouses, devoted children and trustworthy friends."

Hearing that the Mother of the Universe was manifesting in a visible body, sages and cosmic intelligences like Brahma rushed to the scene. Catching a glimpse of the Mother's supremely beautiful face, and seeing the magnificent city which the cosmic architect Vishvakarma had instantly built for her, Brahma the Creator thought, "It is no more appropriate for a woman to rule such a city alone than for a king to rule a kingdom without a queen. The Supreme Goddess must have a husband, but who in all these worlds is worthy of her? Only Lord Shiva himself, but he sits dirty and disheveled in meditation, so she may not be attracted to him."

Sensing the Creator's thoughts, a portion of Shiva's awareness materialized before Brahma's eyes and turned to look at Lalita. What a scene: Shiva, the ascetic God who had incinerated Kama, the force of lust, found himself melting like butter in the hot sun before the bewitching form of the Mother of the Universe, who embodied in herself the very essence of sexual power. The Lord of the Yogis immediately assumed a body so beautiful even Brahma, the grandfather of the worlds, was captivated. Stunningly handsome, draped in gorgeous robes, jewels and garlands, Shiva was breathtaking.

Smiling, the Goddess announced, "Bright beings, whatever I say or do is according to my own will alone. Whichever man accepts me as his wife must also accept my complete independence." Saying this, she pulled the garland from her neck and tossed it high into the sky. It circled the gods, streamed around the ecliptic, and finally landed around Shiva's neck. In this beautiful garlanded form he became known as Kameshvara, the Lord of Passionate Love. He and Lalita were immediately united in marriage, to the great delight of the deities and saints.

There was no honeymoon. The Divine Mother had promised to free the demi-gods from fear, so immediately she set out to meet Bhanda in battle. The *Brahmanda Purana* lovingly describes the powerful military commanders who accompanied her, all awesome and intelligent *shaktis*, demi-goddesses eager to free the world from evil, riding in extraordinary chariots the likes of which had never been seen on earth. This section of the scripture too is entirely yogic: the *shaktis* are the innate energies of the subtle body, and their chariots are the *yantras* or sacred mandalas in which these energies embody themselves when their images are worshiped with reverence.

WOMEN WARRIORS

When Bhanda heard an army of women was approaching his city, he howled with laughter. His younger brother, however, soberly cautioned, "It is Shakti (divine power) which gives every victory. We have reason to fear anyone who becomes a seat of that energy. Don't underestimate these soldiers because they're women. Remember that in former times, a divinely inspired woman named Chandika killed the great warriors Mahisha, Sumbha and Nisumbha. Let's find out who these women are before we counterattack."

Bhanda would have none of it. "The gods are so terrified, they don't have the courage to come themselves! They're sending an army of girls against us! I have so many well trained soldiers, they could drink an entire sea if they were thirsty enough. We'll have no trouble with this pathetic excuse for an army!" Unfortunately for Bhanda, he overlooked a fact reasserted again and again in Hindu art and scripture: that in all of nature there is no force more indomitable than a woman fighting for justice.

With tremendous enthusiasm, the author of the *Brahmanda Purana* details the ensuing rout, as the women warriors decimate Bhanda's clueless male troops. Every phase of the battle represents a stage of spiritual self-purification. In one episode, for example, the demon general Balahaka overcame Lalita's *shaktis* with a boon he long ago received from the Sun God. Whenever he looked at an enemy with anger, rays of hot light shot from his eyes, paralyzing his opponent. Seeing many of the *shaktis* overcome by this force, the demi-goddess Tiraskaranika descended on the general, firing an arrow that covered his eyes with an impenetrable veil. While he staggered in confusion, she lopped off his head. In case anyone has missed the point of the allegory—that anger is such a debilitating force it can stop the purifying energies of the Higher Self in their tracks—the author pointedly explains that it was actually Balahaka's own wrath which blinded him.

Bhanda turned to his chief sorcerer for help. Grinning maliciously, the sorcerer prepared a special *yantra,* a geometric design infused with curses, and hurled it into the camp of the *shaktis.* Suddenly the demi-goddesses, always eager to serve Lalita, found themselves giving in to lassitude and despair. "Why should we fight injustice in the world? What difference will all our self-sacrificing efforts make in the end? We're throwing our lives away for nothing. And why should we practice such strict self-disciplines? We're not going to become enlightened in this lifetime anyway. Why not relax and enjoy life a little? Besides, we're so tired! Why should we be vigilant every moment? Let's get some sleep!"

Of all the *shaktis,* only the two supreme commanders, Dandanatha (breath control) and Mantrini, (the power of mantra) were so firmly established in their spiritual practices that they remained unaffected by discouragement or sloth. They hurried to Lalita to report, "Empress, the demon army is attacking and our soldiers are sleeping!"

Lalita was not in the least distressed, but began to laugh! From her beautiful peals of laughter a huge, ungainly form began to materialize. He had the muscular body of a very strong, but very corpulent, young man, and the head of an elephant. This is how Ganesha, the popular elephant-headed god of Hinduism, was born.

Highly intelligent like all elephants, Ganesha immediately sensed what was wrong. Pausing only a moment to bow to his Mother, he quickly sprinted away to locate the evil *yantra* which had cast a stuporous spell over the *shaktis.* He found it almost immediately and smashed it to pieces with his tusk. Instantly the women warriors leaped to their feet, eager to resume battle. Lalita was so delighted with her son's excellent service, she granted him the boon that he would be worshiped first before any of the other gods. That is why, to this day, whenever Hindus begin a worship service, they always start by honoring Ganesha.

Ganesha represents firm determination. Whenever the mind is resolute, all obstacles are overcome, enthusiasm is sustained, and victory is ensured. The root of determination is self confidence and good humor.

Bhanda then decided to attack by night, a tactic completely against the code of Hindu chivalry. Noting that the Goddess Lalita always sent her *shaktis* to fight while she herself remained hidden in the background, observing and controlling all their motions, he planned to surround her in the darkness and lead the attack from behind. Through darkness so deep it swallowed the entire earth, Bhanda sent his black-armored troops to capture Lalita. This surprise attack caught the *shaktis* off guard; many of them were seriously wounded. Then the undying cosmic intelligences who bask eternally in the Goddess's glow drew their bows of *prana,* breath or life energy, and staved off the attack. Injured women warriors were carried into Lalita's presence where a loving glance from her eyes, ever moist with mercy, instantly healed their wounds.

The text is warning that selfish desires and self-defeating impulses can invade even very advanced states of meditation. When these distractions are experienced, the seeker is advised to practice *pranayama,* breath control, to still the disturbances in the mind. And at any time one feels shaken or despairing or defeated, withdrawing one's awareness and placing oneself fully in the light of the Goddess, the divine consciousness within which is the source of all healing power, will restore one's faith and energy.

Mantrini and Dandanatha, Lalita's two generals, were disturbed by the near success of Bhanda's last assault, and analyzed their defensive strategy carefully. They quickly saw, and repaired, weak areas in their bulwarks, representing those aspects of our personalities with which we subvert our own best efforts. All parts of our being must be balanced and in harmony if we are to avoid defeating ourselves. The further one progresses in spiritual life, the higher the stakes become. Vedic literature is replete with stories of great yogis who advanced to very high stages of spiritual practice, only to tumble to subhuman levels because some shadow in their minds had never been exposed to the light of self awareness.

THE INNER LIGHT

Mantrini and Dandanatha decided to protect Lalita with a rampart of blazing fire. Only a tiny gate would be allowed in the rampart, where the Goddess's forces could come and go. The entrance would be guarded day and night by powerful *shaktis* who never sleep. Thus the abode of the Supreme Consciousness was surrounded by a garland of impassable flames.

This ring of fire is often mentioned in the yogic literature, where it has variously been described as a golden disk concealing the innermost truth, a shining globe at the end of a dark tunnel which everyone glimpses at the time of death (and through whose blazing light only enlightened souls can pass), or as the Inner Sun. It is not a metaphor but a literal experience reported by many advanced meditators. An American-born yogi named Bhagavan Das, who spent years in India studying with Hindu and Tibetan masters, described his encounter with the Inner Light as one of the supreme experiences of his life. It appeared to him in deep meditation, he told me, blazing so brightly his entire mind field was suffused with a light of such intensity it was blinding, as if he were gazing directly into a thousand sunrises. This inner dawning propelled him into the highest state of ecstacy he'd ever experienced.

Two thousand years ago, Plutarch, a priest of Apollo at the temple of Delphi, described the process most of us undergo at death:

> At first the soul wanders in confusion and fear along exhausting paths which seem to lead nowhere. Then a brilliant,

extraordinary light appears to meet him, filled with everything beautiful and auspicious. If he has lived a pure life, perfecting himself spiritually, he passes through this light effortlessly, achieving the goal of human existence, and communes with it in holiness. Below him those who flee the light due to their lack of purity and faith, pass through a deep fog into purgatory. Eventually they are reborn in a body to try again to find their way back to the light.

It is not uncommon for people who have had near death experiences to report that they experienced this blissful light. Yogis and yoginis consciously cultivate this vision of light in their meditation. Shaktas explain that this light is one's own Higher Self, the footstool of the Goddess.

The holiest of all verses in the *Vedas,* the Gayatri mantra, invokes the enlightening wisdom of this very experience. "We meditate on the Inner Sun, the most splendid light in all the worlds. Please illumine our hearts and minds, and make our lives radiant!" This prayer has been chanted daily by orthodox Hindus for more than six thousand years.

The entrance to the realm beyond this light is said to be accessible to those who never sleep. This sounds mythical, but again the meaning is literal. Under laboratory conditions, yogis have demonstrated the ability to remain fully conscious, aware of everything occurring in the room around them, while scientific instrumentation unambiguously showed that the yogi's brain was in a state of deep sleep. The ability to remain lucid not only during dreams but even in deep sleep is one of the better known powers the Goddess grants advanced meditators in the yogic tradition.

Next Bhanda sent his own sons into battle, certain these exceptional warriors he had trained himself would be able to vanquish the Goddess. As they reached for their bows and arrows he apologized for sending them on such a demeaning mission, to capture a helpless woman!

Learning that Bhanda's sons were poised for battle, Bala's face lit with excitement. She ran to Lalita begging, "Mother, mother, please let me fight the demon princes!" Bala was Lalita's nine-year-old daughter—in fact the Sanskrit word *bala* means "young girl." Lalita swept her daughter up in her arms and laughed, "Darling, you're much too young! You've barely finished your training and you don't have any experience in combat. Let powerful *shaktis* like Mantrini and Dandanatha fight instead. You're the most precious thing in the world to me—let me take care of the fighting."

Bala was adamant. "Mommy, I'm going to fight!" Her eyes twinkling with delight, Lalita dressed her daughter in her own armor and gave her her own weapons. Mantrini and Dandanatha were horrified to see Bala heading into battle but were unable to stop the determined girl.

Riding in a palanquin, Bala unleashed a shower of arrows on Bhanda's unsuspecting sons. Soon all of them lay dead and the young girl returned home in triumph. During the entire encounter, Mantrini and Dandanatha never left Bala's side. They allowed her to fight her own battle, but were ready to swoop to her protection at a split second's notice if the need arose.

Readers may object, "Wait a minute! Lalita just got married a few days ago! How can she already have a nine-year-old daughter?" And yet, who do you imagine you are if you don't recognize at once that *you* are Bala? Lalita is the all pervading consciousness/power which creates, sustains, and annihilates the cosmos. You are her dearest child, eager, like her, to express your creativity, to maintain your personal universe, and you put away your toys when you lose interest. Lalita redresses evil on a cosmic scale; you fight for what you believe is right on whatever scale you can manage. If you have truly passed victoriously through the tests metaphorically described as battles in this text, then you are no longer a human personality adrift in an ocean of births and deaths, but truly are the Goddess Bala, that is, the Higher Self, a glorious, infinitesimal portion of your Mother, the Self of the Universe.

Whether you are male or female, you are the daughter of the Goddess. The Divine Awareness which birthed you from her own limitless being loves you more than you are capable of conceiving. You ride into the "battle" of earthly experience in your palanquin— your physical body—but all the while Mantrini and Dandanatha, the protective energies of the Mother of the Universe, are watching over and protecting you. They will allow you to make your own mistakes, if necessary, but at the end of the battle they will most assuredly carry you home to your Mother.

But in this vast and fearsome universe, there may be forces so powerful that neither you nor even puissant cosmic deities can overcome them. Bhanda—the reproductive energy of nature gone bad, the desire to merge with another turned to self-aggrandizement, the sacred magnetism of love used to manipulate or destroy, love subsumed in lust—can be so overpoweringly compelling that even great saints are humbled by its ferocity. As Bhanda himself finally approaches to do battle, Lalita at last rises from her throne in the *sahasrara chakra*. The gateway in the circle of fire which keeps all profane thoughts from entering the holy of holies spontaneously widens, and the Mother of the Universe herself descends into physical consciousness to meet her greatest foe. When we have done all we can do to purify ourselves, when we have fought and won against the demons inside ourselves, then divine grace descends to destroy the final obstacles between our Higher Self and the Self of All.

The description of this last cosmic battle is amazing. Bhanda attacks the Mother of the Worlds with arrows of fear, illness, materialism, apathy, and destruction of the sacred teachings. Lalita responds with arrows of courage, vibrant health, spiritual insight, active compassion, and selfless, enlightened spiritual mentors. Finally Bhanda unleashes all the forces of perdition, designed to rip human society to pieces. From the tips of the Goddess's fingers emerge the *avatars,* incarnations of God like Lord Rama and Lord Krishna who manifest on earth to restore order and righteousness.

At the culmination of this final confrontation Bhanda launches his most terrifying missile, the one called *mahamoha,* "the supreme delusion" that anything exists anywhere in the universe that is not completely sacred. Lalita blasts it to pieces with her own missile called *shambhava,* "divine awareness." And then the Mother of the Universe overcame Bhanda, selfish lust born from the ashes of love, with the most powerful force in the universe, *maha kameshvara,* "pure divine love."

In the conflagration Bhanda's capital city Shunyaka was also destroyed. It contained everything Bhanda had ever won for himself. Its name means simply "emptiness."

Bhanda's fatal error was believing himself invincible because he had been granted the boon to drain half his enemy's might in any encounter. Since he never made the effort to understand who Lalita was, and never realized that she is the Para Shakti, the Supreme Primordial Energy, it didn't dawn on him that half of infinity is still infinity. No matter how much energy he drained from the Mother of the Universe, her resources would remain inexhaustible.

The gods all rushed to congratulate Lalita on this great victory. But Brahma the Creator had one more item on his agenda. "Mother, everyone in the world is celebrating your victory. Everyone that is, except one desolate, grieving widow. Please have pity on Rati, who weeps day and night. Some years ago her husband Kama, intending only good, fired an arrow of sexual arousal at Lord Shiva. The Lord became angry and burned Kama to ashes. Now you have destroyed even the demon who arose from those ashes! But without sexual energy, the physical universe will collapse. How can more bodies be provided for the trillions upon trillions of souls who still want to incarnate in matter to fulfill their physical desires?"

Smiling, the Mother of the Universe swept the cosmos with her sidelong glance. From that loving glance a form began to coalesce. At that moment the widow Rati felt someone materializing near her. There was her husband Kama, in a body even more handsome than his last one, rushing to embrace her. As the God of Desire and the Goddess of Romance threw themselves into each others' arms, all the denizens of heaven applauded enthusiastically.

"Mother, you have restored my life!" Kama gratefully called out to Lalita. "I will be your servant forever! Please tell me how I can serve you!"

Lalita laughed and laughed. "My darling son, you have my blessings and my protection. Go about your business, enchanting the entire world. Tease those who repudiate your power by withdrawing their joyfulness. Embarrass those who believe they have mastered you by drawing them into scandal. And fill the lives of my devotees with delight! One more thing: there is a very great soul you will have to face again."

Kama's handsome face lit up with mischief. "Yes Mother, I understand." Accompanied by the spring breeze and the fragrant scent of flowers, he returned to the grove where the greatest of all ascetics, the three-eyed Lord Shiva, was still ensconced in meditation. This time Kama's aim was true: his flower arrow pierced the Lord's heart. Shiva jolted to physical consciousness, opened his eyes, and in the far distance saw a young woman named Parvati fervently meditating on his lotus feet. He fell in love instantly. Though he was beside himself with desire, he realized he couldn't make this woman his wife without carefully testing her first. But that's another story.

Shiva is pure, unalloyed consciousness, which contains within it infinite potential but which in itself has no desire to procreate. Indeed, the highest states of consciousness are so blissful that some yogis who attain them lose the desire to return to the material worlds, where their blessing energy is sorely needed. Shiva is, in effect, the universe before the beginning of time as we know it, a single, incredibly concentrated point (Sanskrit *bindu*) containing an incalculable amount of heat (Sanskrit *tapas,* which also means concentration or asceticism) and energy (*shakti*). At some point billions of years ago, a vector of energy (Kama's arrow) created an imbalance in this immeasurable point of energy, causing it to explode, creating the universe we know. (The Vedic scriptures claim there are many other universes, both those which exist invisibly in our own space, and those produced from other *bindus* at inconceivable distances from ours.)

If Shiva is pure consciousness itself, consciousness without an object, Lalita is self-reflective awareness, consciousness which is aware it is conscious, and therefore is capable of conceiving of a universe and holding its evolving form in her timeless awareness. As one of the most loved poems in the Sanskrit language, the *Sundarya Lahari Ananda Lahari* (Waves of Beauty, Waves of Bliss), written by the immortal sage Shankaracharya, puts it:

Without Shakti, Shiva is unable to manifest the universe.
She controls the cosmic forces.
Without the Goddess, God can't lift a finger.

This is not a sectarian snipe at a male image of God, but a profound insight into the mechanics of consciousness and energy. And Lalita, the self-knowing creative intelligence which commands desire to move in the heart of God, also sits enthroned in a mansion built of wish-fulfilling gems, surrounded by the thick bone of our skulls!

The *Brahmanda Purana* concludes with a series of chapters painstakingly describing Lalita's mansion, its antechambers and waiting rooms, as well as the inner compartments where the Goddess herself dwells. Lalita's mansion is the human body. Its inner rooms are the petals of the *sahasrara chakra,* the vortex of psychic energy associated with the roof of the brain. In these rooms the treasures of Spirit are stored, and between these rooms lie passageways into dimensions of being utterly beyond human imagination. For most of us Westerners, these rooms are the stuff of fairy tales. But the adepts of the yoga tradition actually live in these rooms.

THE LIBERATING POWER OF CONSCIOUSNESS

How can the rest of us get there? The arousal of *kundalini,* the liberating power of consciousness, is necessary. *Kundalini* was exhaustively explored in the Indian traditions, including Hinduism, Buddhism, Jainism, and Sikhism, as well as in related traditions such as that of the Chaldeans. The ancient symbol for *kundalini,* two snakes entwined around a central staff topped with two wings, appears not only in the art of India but in extremely ancient Chaldean iconography (circa 2,000 B.C.). In the early Greek tradition also, the God Hermes, representing the *buddhi* or the higher functions of the mind, was shown bearing this caduceus on his flight to the top of Mount Olympus.

The yoga tradition incorporates numerous techniques which mechanically force the *kundalini* energy to rise, including elaborate forms of physical purification, difficult hatha yoga postures, and extremely challenging and potentially dangerous breathing exercises involving retention of the breath for (literally!) hours at a time. Unprepared individuals experimenting with these techniques can harm themselves seriously. An untrained person invites brain damage by holding his or her breath for longer than a few minutes. Yet I myself have sat within inches of yogis in *nirvikalpa samadhi,* watching extremely closely, and can personally attest that these yogis sit without breathing as if they are in some sort of stage of hibernation. By their own report they have drawn their life energies into their spine and up into their brains into the chamber of the Goddess.

It's a remarkable thing to see: their spines are completely erect yet their bodies are relaxed. They sit so completely still it's like watching a rock, or (to give my honest impression) like looking at a corpse, except the corpse is sitting up straight and still has a rosy glow! Their mindfield and physical form are completely still. Under laboratory conditions, some yogis have demonstrated the ability to stop their respiration, heart beat, and even their brain waves! The *Yoga Sutras* actually defines the word yoga as "the cessation of the waves of the mind." In this state the static which usually reverberates in the brain is stilled, and the non-material reality beyond the brain, from which the mind was projected, unimpededly "shines through" into human consciousness.

The *Brahmanda Purana* teaches that there are slower but safer ways of invoking the Goddess Uma in her form as the enlightening energy of kundalini than the extremely challenging techniques practiced by very advanced yogis. We can clear away the demons blocking the flow of enlightened awareness simply by fighting the ordinary battles of our daily lives, rooting out the qualities in our hearts and minds which harm ourselves or others, as well as by directing our natural impulses, such as lust, in a sacred rather than selfish manner.

Bhanda mistakenly believed he could take the Goddess by force. When the Goddess Lalita attacks, her arrows are long-stemmed flowers. She conquers not with violence, but with love. While Bhanda was never admitted into the Goddess's inner chambers, little Bala was allowed in at once because Bala came running with innocent love. When we approach the Mother with that kind of pure devotion, she scoops us up in her arms and sends Mantrini and Dandanatha to fight our demons for us.

Years ago many of my friends were enchanted by a popular movie about Saint Francis of Assisi. I myself flinched at the scenes in which Francis was supposed to be having a vision of Jesus. We in the West have so completely lost touch with our mystical traditions that the film makers actually portrayed Francis hyperventilating during this mystical epiphany! Mystics of all traditions report that in the deepest states of spiritual ecstasy, the breath slows and finally stops. But it's not necessary to practice holding one's breath in order to see the Divine Mother. Just love the Divine Mother. The breath will stop by itself—safely and naturally. The Mother herself will guard and protect your body while your awareness remains fixed on her form, her mantra, her pure beingness. Allow your *chakras* to turn upwards and bloom spontaneously, nurtured in the soil of your faith and devotion. They turn naturally toward the radiance of the Inner Sun, the Mother's glittering footstool.

Readers familiar with the history of Western philosophy will remember that there was a tremendous sense of excitement among the Neoplatonic philosophers of the fourth and fifth centuries, a sort of spiritual renaissance, as the practice of theurgy was reintroduced to the Greeks by Chaldean adepts. Theology means literally "God talk" but theurgy means "God work" or "working to become God," and the Greeks were galvanized to make the transition from merely talking about God to actually experiencing divine being. Unfortunately these techniques were soon violently suppressed. But theurgy was never lost in India because from remotest antiquity the Hindus understood that the Divine Mother is not someone other than ourselves, but the very root of our being. Therefore the practices of yoga, which deliver us to our innermost Self, carry us into the presence of the living Goddess, our source and essence.

All three major Western faiths, Christianity, Islam and Judaism, take a sharply opposing view. From the perspective of their orthodox adherents, claiming that we are in any sense "one with God" is revoltingly sacrilegious. Only in Christianity was one individual, Jesus the Nazarene, allowed to get away with flatly stating, "I and the Father are one." When Jesus elaborated to his disciples, "Become ye perfect, as the Father is perfect," he was encouraging them to embrace their own union with divine being, but this most pivotal of Jesus's teachings has been ignored in the West. As is the case with so many of Jesus's instructions, preachers today teach exactly the opposite: that it is impossible for us to become perfect because only God is perfect, and we are definitely not God!

The radically opposing worldviews of East and West have dramatic consequences. For example, in the West a saint is someone who loves God and serves humanity. In India a saint not only worships the divine and serves selflessly, but she herself consciously becomes divine. We all are divine, according to the Goddess tradition, but the saints actually experience their divinity moment to moment—they have purified themselves to a degree where the

Inner Light suffuses their entire being and radiates outward in an unending stream of blessings to those around them.

The notion of "becoming God" sets off alarm bells in the West, and for good reasons. We think of David Koresch claiming, "I am Jesus Christ," and shudder. But in the course of the millennia, Hindus have been around the block with this one, and have long since learned to distinguish the genuine article from the fraud and the psychotic. Koresch is unlikely to have gathered a following in India because the Hindus judge their saints not by how large the would-be saint's ego is, but by how small his or her ego has become. When Anasuya Devi, the late beloved saint of Andhra Pradesh, was asked how she experienced her unity with the Divine Mother, she replied, "I am not anything you are not. It doesn't appear to me that I am greater than you. God does not exist separately anywhere. You are all God."

The *Vedas* say, "When the sage sees the Self in all beings, and all beings in the Self, it is impossible for him to hate anyone." When one truly recognizes the divinity within oneself, one recognizes the divinity in all things, and the sort of maniacal ego inflation we see in Jim Jones types does not occur.

Recently while I was lecturing on the American East Coast, a gentleman introduced himself, in total sincerity, as Jesus Christ. We chatted for a while and it turned out several years previously he spontaneously began having deeply moving—and probably completely genuine—mystical experiences of peace and bliss. These confused and frightened him because he had been raised to believe we are all sinners, and only Jesus is capable of the union with divine being he was beginning to experience. After wrestling with this conundrum for some years, he finally realized he must be Jesus born again, and that God had sent him to destroy the earth in order to inaugurate the millennium prophesied in the Bible. It saddens me that for all our material advantages, we Westerners live in a world so spiritually impoverished that instead of leading a soul to increasing altruism and beatitude, our faulty understanding of mystical states can drive us into psychosis.

In the mystical literature of India's Goddess tradition, *kundalini* is said to work itself upwards through the lower *chakras* or levels of consciousness preoccupied with self preservation, sensuality and self assertion, into higher *chakras* or centers concerned with altruistic efforts, the arts and aesthetics, knowledge and transcendence. The mystical marriage of the Goddess Uma/*kundalini* with Lord Shiva occurs when awareness stabilizes in the highest portion of the subtle body, in the Higher Self. The following story makes an extremely important point about this process.

Many thousands of years ago, Uma was born on earth as Parvati, daughter of the Himalayas (i.e., a yogini). From her earliest childhood, Parvati wanted only one thing: Lord Shiva, the embodiment of absolute consciousness, as her husband. When she was still a young girl she retired into the forest to perform intense asceticism in order to acquire sufficient merit to earn this greatest of all marriages: union with divine being itself.

Taking her seat in a secluded clearing, Parvati made a fearsome vow. "I will not move from my meditation seat until Lord Shiva appears to me and offers his love. If for even one moment my mind wanders from the feet of my Lord, may I lose the fruit of my entire penance and lose him forever!"

Parvati sat completely still, her mind totally absorbed in devotion to Shiva, for day after day, year after year. Terrific monsoon winds and rains did not disturb her meditation. A herd of elephants stampeded the clearing; Parvati didn't flinch. A roaring forest fire devoured the trees around her, roasting her body with its fierce heat, but Parvati remained unmoved. Though the years passed, hunger and thirst, sleep and lust, impatience and despair, could not find any distracted area of her mind to enter through.

Then one day in the distance Parvati heard the piercing scream of a terrified child.

There was not one moment's hesitation. Instantly Parvati was on her feet, racing to help. In a nearby stream she saw the young child being attacked by a crocodile. Immediately Parvati leapt into the water to try to save the child. Astonishingly, her feet didn't get wet. Instead the entire scene dissolved away and Lord Shiva himself stood before her eyes.

"Parvati," Shiva said sternly, *"this* was your final test. You had sworn never to allow anything to distract you from worshiping me."

Then a smile broke across the Lord's beautiful face. "You sacrificed everything, even union with me, to help the helpless. My darling, today at last you have proven yourself truly worthy to be my wife."

One-pointed spiritual practice leads to Shiva, divine awareness, but active compassion *is* the Divine Mother. Compassion is the consort of enlightened awareness. Altruism is the natural expression of the Goddess acting through us in the world.

Mother delights in watching us play with the toys she's given us. But there comes a time when she expects us to put our toys away and learn our lessons. As we mature spiritually, Mother prepares us for our work in the world. From Shiva's perspective the crocodiles are an illusion from start to finish, but it's our job to leap into the stream and fight them anyway.

According to the Goddess tradition, if we do our job well and learn the lessons we were sent here to learn, the day comes when we too will celebrate the Inner Marriage. Then we are offered the choice to joyously continue participating in the dream of existence in this universe, to move on to another subtler universe, or step out of these universes altogether. Wherever we choose to go, we don't really go anywhere. We are now exactly where we've always been and where we always will be, resting in the widest lap in the universe.

Kundalini Stavah:
PRAYER FOR
THE AWAKENING OF CONSCIOUSNESS

Divine consciousness ever seeks
    to rescue helpless souls like me
    from life's recurring deaths.
Mother Kundalini, consort of the Self-existent,
    lead me to immortality!
Shining red one, who takes the form of a snake,
    cool moon glow of deathlessness,
    see how I suffer!
My body reeks of mortality.
Irradiate me with your ambrosial beams.
Sincere aspirants who honestly face their faults
    achieve the supreme victory
    through the science of kundalini.

Abandoning the kingdom of death
    they find their way to the city of liberation.
You tear out desires by their roots
    from your home at the root of the spine.
The wise ones bow before your coiled form,
    praising you with sacred songs.
When you refuse to move from the base of the spine,
    you make even the greatest beings slaves
    of their basest impulses.
But when you rise through the three worlds,
    piercing the knots of the subtle body,
    you destroy the roots of bondage.

I bow to the liberating power of consciousness
    who bestows enlightenment as she rises
    through the subtle bodies of purified souls,
    but who causes havoc when she flashes
    in the subtle bodies of the unprepared.

You are the queen of the life force.
You radiate bliss.
You who travel the subtle path, please bless me!
You are unfailingly gracious to those who meditate
    with total concentration.
Those who take refuge in you
    find their way to the heaven within.
With deepest reverence, I bow to Mother Kundalini.
Please lift my limited awareness
    from the empty hovel of my egotism
    to the thousand-chambered mansion
    of divine consciousness!

Reclaiming the Goddess Tradition of the West:
Our Own Living Goddess

THE MIDNIGHT SUN

My family is from a tiny Norwegian island called Anderjå which juts up out of the icy waters several hundred miles north of the Arctic Circle. As a child I would sit on the pier overlooking the fjord at midnight, and watch the sun bounce off the North Sea, dipping down toward the ocean, then arcing slowly back up into the sky. Summer was my favorite time of year because the sun never set; in the middle of the night you could sit outside reading a book without having to turn on a light. Our window shades were black—not white like the ones I use now in America—to keep out the blazing sunlight while my parents were trying to sleep.

When I told Swami Rama Bharati, the first yogi I ever met, that I was Norwegian, he laughed and shouted, "We're cousins!" He was referring to our shared Indo-European heritage. Yet the light of that spectacular heritage, which shone so brightly in the Hellenistic world, flickered out in the first few centuries of our era. In Greek times many slaves could read; after the West entered its Dark Age, even emperors were illiterate. Astronomy, medicine and the other sciences collapsed, and the status of women (who were priestesses and professors in the Hellenistic period) crumbled. A new religion had caught the West in a stranglehold, reaching even Norway by 1000 A.D. The priests of this religion recited the teachings of its founder in a language common people couldn't understand. This was useful in preventing Europe's beleaguered peasants from learning enough about Jesus's words to realize that many of their leaders, both political and spiritual, were disregarding Christ's actual teachings at every turn. Unfortunately, this continues to the present day, as politicians posing as Christians self-righteously press on the American public an agenda which is in almost every detail the opposite of Jesus'.

The worst tragedy of Europe's Dark Age was not only that thinking was no longer allowed (questioning the church was a capital offense), but that direct personal exploration of mystical states was strictly forbidden. To this day most Christian churches actively discourage involvement in Eastern-style meditation techniques, techniques which help one develop and deepen one's connection with Spirit. Of course not even the church could keep the human soul in chains—some lone saints made extraordinary spiritual breakthroughs. Those who couched their experiences in Christian terms were canonized (after they were safely dead); those who didn't, were executed. Perhaps the inevitable result of severing so many people from their inner spiritual roots was that when Western science began to flourish again in the 17th century, it quickly became completely soulless.

Not surprisingly, what sparked the Renaissance was renewed contact with the East. Indian science and mathematics made its way to Europe through Arab intermediaries. The works of Plato and the Hermetic philosophers of Alexandria, so astonishingly Hindu in tone and content, were devoured by spiritually impoverished Europeans. For the sun of spiritual knowledge had never set in India. Even in the darkest night of aggressive foreign occupation, yoga science continued to flourish in the subcontinent, mystical experience was never anathematized, and the midnight sun of the Goddess tradition shone resplendently every hour of the day.

In India the Sun Goddess is called Savitri. Our earth circles her every year in respectful circumambulation. She sets at the moment of our birth and rises again at the moment of our death, when we see her shining before us as resplendently as a thousand sunrises. The Shakta tradition teaches us to walk in her light every hour of our lives. May that divine Inner Sun illuminate our minds!

The Portal of the Goddess

The mares carry me from the kingdom of night
toward the land of light to which I aspire.

Led by the daughters of the Sun, eagerly I come
    to the inner gate I have so long desired.
The women ask the mistress to allow me to pass;
    and—at last—I step inside.

The Goddess greets me with love.
"Young one," she says, "welcome.
You've traveled far from the paths of men
    to find admittance at my door.
I will tell you the true nature of things,
    so different from the common lore.
Then you must return to the world of night,
    bringing the light I will reveal,
    teaching others to tell aright
    the real and the unreal."

In this poem, one of the most famous and influential in world history, the Goddess goes on to unveil her innermost truths. She begins before the beginning, with the mind shattering question of why anything should exist at all. The aspirant who has found his way to her portal believes that he exists, that the world exists, and that the Goddess exists, yet what does he really know? What does he know about existence itself?

"If nothing exists," the Goddess laughs, "we wouldn't be here to ask about it. Therefore there is one self-evident reality at the root of all experience: existence exists."

Could existence have had a beginning? No, for it could not have emerged from non-existence. Nothing cannot produce anything. Being is, was, and ever will be simply what it is. It can't change, because then it would stop being what it is. It would partake of non-existence.

This unchanging substratum of pure being, however, is not the experience of most people. Humans find themselves caught in a universe of continual flux, where thoughts and things, people and planets, pass in and out of existence. This flux, the Goddess explains, is an illusion produced by the tendency of human minds to create dualities, to feel hot or cold where there is only what is, to find pain or pleasure where there is only what is, to see good or evil where there is only what is.

"Use your intelligence to penetrate the veil of duality and uncover the unchanging unity beneath appearances," the Goddess commands.

This, of course, is the very heart of Shakta understanding. "Being" (Shiva) is infinite, unchanging self-existence. Shiva is revealed by Shakti, the limitless power of consciousness which is the root of both *maya* (the capacity to perceive multiplicity, the "thousand things" around us) and *mukti* (enlightened perception of universal unity). One of the paths to enlightened awareness is *Jnana Yoga,* the way of discriminating intellect in which the aspirant trains herself to distinguish between the eternal and the ephemeral, "the real and the unreal." *Jnana Yoga* is the very path this poem urges us to tread.

But the poem wasn't written in India. It was composed in Greece by one of the most influential thinkers of all time, Parmenides of Elea (born about 515 B.C.). Parmenides has been almost completely forgotten today, but for nearly a thousand years he was remembered by the Greeks and Romans as one of their greatest sages.

Incidentally, Parmenides' teacher was a Pythagorean. Numerous scholars have noted the astonishing similarities between many of Pythagoras' doctrines and Hindu thought. The possibility that Parmenides was indirectly influenced by the Goddess tradition of India—the central tenets of which his famous poem articulates—remains open.

It's fun to watch Western scholars struggle with Parmenides today. One of the questions they wrestle with is, who is this Goddess of the inner gate? Most scholars admit they don't have a clue. And many of them complain that all this "being" and "nonbeing" business is unintelligible. It's clear that Parmenides was taken very seriously by generation after generation of Greek intellectuals, but Western scholars today aren't quite sure what he was saying.

Let's make an educated guess: Parmenides was saying the same thing thoughtful devotees of the Mother of the Universe were saying in India and China, the Americas, Africa and Chaldea. Even today the Kogi tribes of Tairona, the last remnants of the priesthood of pre-Columbian South America, preserve a similar understanding of

Aluna, the Cosmic Mother, as the yogis and yoginis in the Himalayas. It appears the ancient tradition of the Mother was astonishingly uniform almost everywhere on earth. It was not primarily a fertility cult. If anything, it was primarily a cult of consciousness, a peering into the conscious heart of reality and into the creative power of its eternally beating heart.

THE MOTHER OF THE GODS

Did the forebears of Western civilization share the Shakta's view of the Great Mother? Scholars today claim we can't know what the ancient mystery "cults" of Europe and the Mediterranean taught. Their esoteric teachings, if they were anything more than fertility mumbo jumbo anyway, have long since vanished.

But important and extremely intriguing clues about the nature of the Goddess in Western mystery religions have survived. Let's turn, for example, to Emperor Julian Flavius, the last great champion of classical Western culture, whose tragic assassination in 363 A.D. pitched Europe into the Dark Ages. Julian partially pulls aside the veil of the Goddess in his remarkable essay, "On the Mother of the Gods." He begins by relating how Cybele came to Rome. The Romans appealed to the Oracle at Delphi for help in their conflict with Carthage, and were advised by the high priestess of Apollo to propitiate the Phrygian Goddess Cybele. The Phrygians were unenthused about parting with their Goddess, but finally placed her *murti,* the image of the Goddess in which her living essence had been infused, on a boat for Rome.

Cybele was well aware that many Romans were skeptical about her powers, and decided to teach them a lesson. Some miles before reaching Rome, her boat stopped moving forward. Frantic Romans sailors tried to dislodge the ship, but it wouldn't budge. This was extremely inauspicious: the Goddess of Victory was refusing to enter their city!

The Romans were sure this disaster couldn't be their fault, and decided the problem must lie with Claudia, a priestess who had been chosen to serve Cybele in her new Roman temple. She must have broken her vows, incurring the Goddess's wrath. When Claudia heard the rumors, she rushed to the site. Tying her belt around the ship's prow, she called out, "Mother of the Gods, if I am innocent of the charges the Romans have laid against me, enter the city!" She tugged on her belt and instantly the boat lurched forward. Walking along the river bank, the priestess effortlessly pulled the huge ship down the Tiber all the way to Rome. After this the chastened Romans had tremendous faith in Cybele; in fact they made her their national Goddess. (Incidentally, with Cybele's help, the Romans won the war against Carthage.)

Emperor Julian remarks that in his own day, despite the fact that this episode was recorded in authoritative histories of early Rome, some young men insisted it couldn't be true, that only "old women" could believe such a tale. Although they had eyes, Julian commented dryly, these young cynics were unable to see. The "old women," like the "daughters of the Sun" who led Parmenides into the living presence of the Goddess, were able to penetrate realms of reality which remained closed to those who relied exclusively on the evidence of their senses and the dictates of their rational minds.

The central myth of Cybele is that she fell in love with a handsome human named Attis, and they had a glorious love affair. However, while the Goddess was attending to her numerous divine duties, Attis slipped off into a cavern where he enjoyed a tryst with a nymph. In retaliation, Cybele had her lover castrated. A eunuch now, Attis returned to Cybele, and they lived happily ever after.

To scholars of ancient mythologies, this bizarre myth transparently represents a fertility rite. Attis' castration must represent autumn; his reunion with Cybele must represent spring. To feminists, however, the myth is unmistakably the expression of women's rage at male infidelity. Interestingly, Emperor Julian—who was himself an initiate of the mystery religions—didn't see the story in these terms at all. How did the Divine Mother's Roman initiates two thousand years ago understand her and her mysterious ways?

The Mother of the Gods, Julian explained, is the eternal matrix from which all grades of consciousness in the universe, including that of the gods themselves, emerge. She is a virgin though ever united in marriage with the Supreme God, without beginning herself though the source of everything perceptible and imperceptible, the mistress of all life.

Now this divine creative consciousness, Julian goes on to say, loves the soul and "commanded him to associate with none other than herself." Together they remained in an epiphany of bliss. However, the soul allowed himself to be enticed by a nymph in a cavern, that is by the seductive beauty of the world of matter, and soon found himself trapped by his desires in the cold, dark, damp cave of a physical body. Taking pity on Attis, the Mother of the Gods decided to rescue her lost lover. She sent her servant to castrate him, that is, to stop him from any further "generation in matter." That is to say, she sent a guru to teach the soul how to stop generating more *karma*, which would enmesh him even more deeply in *maya*.

Hearing the triumphant blast of Cybele's trumpet, Attis loses his desire to engage in worldly affairs. In a shock of recognition, the soul realizes what a terrible mistake he's made, remembers his previous state of glory in higher reaches of consciousness, and rushes back to his one true desire, the Mother of the Universe, who joyfully crowns her prodigal lover with a tiara of stars.

You would certainly think no man would rush back to a woman who's just had him emasculated, yet the myth insists that Attis hurries home, where he and Cybele are joyously reunited and resume their affair. How can a eunuch resume a sexual relationship? The truth, as Julian makes explicit, is that the story has nothing to do with sex. It's about the liberation of the soul. "The trumpet Attis heard immediately after his castration is a signal to us also, who like Attis, having flown from heaven, have fallen to the earth," Julian concludes. By this myth "the gods exhort us to quickly return to the essential unity in ourselves. What greater joy can there be than when the soul flies from the infinite world with its ceaseless storms, to the One itself? In this manner the Mother of the Gods reabsorbed the soul into her own being."

"Always be alert when you encounter ancient myths that, on their surface, don't appear to make sense," Julian advised, "for the ancients concealed their wisdom under a veil of nonsensical fables, so that their paradoxes would propel our minds past the constraints of logic to direct insight into reality." Aristotle concurred, explaining that the masters of the ancient mystery religions didn't teach analytically, but forced their initiates to intuit viscerally. Western scholars today almost universally describe these ancient masters as superstitious, preliterate charlatans who had not yet advanced to the stage of rational thought. The ancients, however, saw themselves as spiritual aspirants who deliberately set out to transcend the limitations of rationality.

"The mind is like a foot ruler," Swami Rama Bharati reiterated again and again. "How can you measure infinity with a ruler? The logical mind will always fail." Instead Swami Rama prescribed devotion, selfless service and, most importantly, the practice of meditation leading to states of awareness transcending thought. Another important part of his prescription was using the most refined portion of one's intelligence to continually distinguish between *sat* (being) and *asat* (non-being). Parmenides was recommending this path back to the Mother 2,500 years ago in Greece, and Emperor Julian struggled to practice this inner discipline 1,500 years ago in Rome. The fact that this fundamental understanding about the unitary nature of reality, and the internal practices needed to experience this oneness, appears and reappears in so many different cultures throughout so many different eras, led the Hindus to call this perennial philosophy the *Sanatana Dharma*, "the eternal religion."

Let's look at another of the mystery religions, the famous Dionysian rites of ancient Greece. At the center of the mystery stands a human woman named Semele, who becomes pregnant by Zeus. Semele dies in childbirth as her son Dionysus is born. But Dionysus is a divine child and restores his mother to life, giving her a new name and taking her to live with the gods. The participants in this "cult" understood that they were Semele, and that through the grace of God divine awareness was growing within them. The process is terribly painful, because for higher consciousness to be born, one's lower self must perish. Once the Higher Self takes birth, however, it illuminates and reintegrates the personality, and life becomes divine.

When Alexander the Great reached India in 327 B.C., he found the Indians worshiping "Dionysus," and cheerfully joined in their rites. Alexander instantly recognized that Shiva was Dionysus, for in those days the Greeks understood that the same God has different names in different cultures. It was centuries later before Christians and Muslims had the insight that because God was called by a different name in their two religions, they were simply going to have to kill each other.

THE MOTHER OF GOD

The representation of divine creative consciousness as the Mother of the Universe has existed in the West from as early as scholars can trace, and even, surprisingly, lies at the root of the Judeo-Christian tradition itself. Few Christians have studied the history of their religion, so most are unaware that from the first few centuries of the Christian era right up through the Middle Ages, there were many different schools of Christianity espousing radically different ideas of who Jesus was and even of how to understand God the Father. Many of the Crusades authorized by the Roman pope were not against "heathens" like the Muslims, but against fellow Christians such as the Cathars and the Hussites—and this in spite of the fact that some of these groups actually adopted lifestyles far closer to Jesus' than did the clerics of Vatican City. Some of these early and medieval Christians had ideas about the Goddess that would amaze and perhaps upset those of us raised as orthodox Christians or Jews today.

For example, the beliefs of the Christian Gnostics, who flourished in the early part of the first millennium, are chronicled on the ancient papyri recovered at Nag Hammadi, Egypt in 1945. These tattered Coptic manuscripts, written at about the same time as the New Testament, show that at least some first and second century Christians conceived of the "Mother of God" in a manner startlingly different than we do today.

The Bible notes that Eve, the mother of humanity, leapt at the chance to eat of the fruit that would "make one wise." God had tried to prevent Adam and Eve from eating of the Tree of Knowledge and the Tree of Life, because if they tasted this fruit they would become equal to God and live forever (Genesis 3:22). Why, I wondered when I first heard these stories as a child, wouldn't God want Eve to be as wise as he was? Why, if he had the power to grant her immortality, would he deny it to her?

The Gnostic Christians asked these same questions, and came to some disturbing conclusions. Noting that the Old Testament deity admits he is a "jealous God," they decided he must want to preserve divine knowledge and the state of deathlessness for himself alone. It bothered the Gnostics that God created human beings only to keep them sequestered in a "paradise" where they would live like animals, as naked foragers. They especially wrestled with the question of how the loving Father of Jesus could be reconciled with an apparently genocidal deity who again and again orders his chosen people to slaughter every man, woman and child in the territories he sends them to invade. The inexplicable and sometimes seemingly diabolical behavior of the Old Testament deity unsettled the Gnostics profoundly.

"I am the Lord thy God. Thou shalt have no other gods before me," God the Father commands in Exodus 20:2-3. Today we Christians hear these words as a ringing declaration of monotheism, the direct revelation of the one true God to his select devotees. The Gnostics, however, felt there was a trace of arrogance in the deity's tone. They were taken aback by the supposedly loving Creator's continual demands for bloody rites, including human sacrifices such as Jephthah's daughter in the Old Testament and Mary's son in the New Testament. Nor could they understand why God would arbitrarily select one group of people as his chosen elect, when the ancient world was filled with many individuals as completely sincere in their spiritual devotion as Abraham had been.

The Gnostics decided the male father God of the Old Testament was a not the highest God after all. The *Hypostasis of the Archons* even claims that God the Father was born when Sophia, the Mother of God, miscarried. "When he opened his eyes he found himself surrounded by limitless unformed matter, and became arrogant. He said, 'I created this! I am God and no one exists but me!'"

The account continues that when God belligerently challenged the surrounding mass of chaotic matter to show him a reality greater than himself, Sophia effortlessly extended her finger, sending a thrill of light through the darkness, but the self-obsessed deity refused to look at it.

There are more surprises in the Gnostic scriptures. According to another Gnostic text, *On the Origin of the World,* Sabaoth, a prototype of Christ, does hear the voice of the Goddess. When he glorifies her, she fills him with light and sends down her daughter Zoe to be his consort and teacher.

The ignorant Father God and his cohorts, the minor deities or "authorities" (Elohim) mentioned in Genesis, initiate an ambitious six-day play to create a kingdom for themselves out of the surrounding mass of unformed matter, complete with a class of menials: humanity. Anticipating this scheme, Zoe laughs, and casts a "drop of light" on the surface of the primeval waters which assumes a female form: Eve. Meanwhile the "authorities" have managed to mold Adam from the dust, though they can't figure out how to animate him till Zoe secretly breathes life into his soulless frame. Congratulating themselves on what they believe is their handiwork, the Elohim take a day off to rest, and Sophia sends Eve as a tutor to awaken Adam's nascent soul. When the authorities spot Adam with a female "light being," they collude to put Adam to sleep, and awaken him with the rather unlikely tale that they created Eve from his rib to be his servant.

Lustful and vengeful, the Elohim decide to rape Eve, hoping to defile her light. The Goddess laughs and assumes the form of the Tree of Knowledge in the Garden of Eden, leaving a phantom semblance of herself for the deities to abuse. But this shadow, the human woman Eve, is not abandoned; in an amazing twist on the Christian redemption story, the Goddess sends a serpent to rescue Eve and Adam from Eden! While orthodox theologians identify the snake in the garden as Satan incarnate, the Gnostics explained that the serpent is a child of the Goddess from a transcendental world beyond the Father's ken, who prefigures Christ. They support this claim by noting that later when an epidemic strikes the Israelites while they spend their 40 years wandering in the desert, they are healed by looking up at the brass image of a serpent hung on a tree, an important clue that the snake in the tree is actually a healer and savior. This is further confirmed for the Gnostics when still later the savior Jesus is also fastened to a tree. ("Be ye wise as serpents," Jesus advises his disciples.)

As the Bible relates, the serpent assures the human Eve that, contrary to God's warning, she will not die if she eats of the Tree of Knowledge, but will become wise, learning to differentiate between good and evil. In the Gnostic account the snake further explains that God tried to frighten Eve from the tree because he knew he would lose his power over her should she become his equal. Eve suspects the serpent is right, and takes the fruit, offering a portion to her husband/disciple. The text recounts that "their mind opened" and Adam and Eve realize that the Creator God is not their benefactor, but the source of their bondage. Having gained the ability to see "good and evil," they are horrified to recognize the ultimate evil in God, a being who wants to prevent them from uncovering their own divinity. Indeed, says the text, "they understood very much."

The Gnostic account goes on to say that, suspecting something has gone awry, God searches in the garden for his former subjects. Realizing that the perfect world he created for himself has been spoiled, God childishly curses creation and his creatures. "There is no blessing from them" the text warns of the wrathful Old Testament God and his ministers. The Elohim bemoan Adam's loss of ignorance, yet this shocking experience awakens them to the fact that there is a power greater than God the Father which has outwitted them. Meanwhile the divine Eve is enraged that the Elohim have cursed the human woman Eve, and comes roaring out of the highest heaven to rout them from their dominions.

This is the apocalyptic vision of the Gnostics:

> The stars will alter their courses, and a tremendous thunder will roar from the place of spirit where the Goddess dwells, far beyond the powers of nature. The Goddess will remove her mantle of wisdom and put on a cloak of uncontrollable fury! Then she will drive out the corrupt gods along with their arrogant Father, throwing them into a bottomless abyss. They will be destroyed by their own injustice!

The Gnostics turn the Bible inside out, praising the intelligence, courage and ultimate divinity of Eve, the most reviled woman in the Western religious tradition! Obviously this version of Eve's spiritual triumph varies dramatically from the story of Eve's "fall" we learned in Sunday school. Eve paid the price for aspiring to divine knowledge within the context of a rigidly patriarchal religious system. Unlike her fellow women aspirants in neighboring Mesopotamian cultures, she was not lauded as a wise woman fit to serve as a priestess, socially and economically independent, and spiritually fecund. Instead she was condemned to be ruled over by her less spiritually perspicacious husband, keeping house and bearing his children in sorrow.

Whether or not we feel comfortable with this astonishing Gnostic vision of Eve, we women in the West are beginning to appreciate that in order to fulfill ourselves socially and spiritually we must, like our mother Eve, also aspire to knowledge, recognizing the good and evil in our social and religious systems, and risking expulsion from the false Eden of the security of traditional sex roles. The Gnostics compel us to look beyond the fatherhood of a jealous, judgmental God, to the wisdom, freedom and transcendence of the Mother of God, Sophia, whose name in the esoteric Jewish system means "Divine Wisdom."

The sharply world-abnegating stance of the Gnostics is not one many of us would necessarily care to emulate, and their critique of the Old Testament is particularly harsh (this despite the fact that most of the Gnostics were Jews). Nevertheless, they represent one of a number of early Christian groups who wrestled with the biblical portrayal of a male God, and who clearly longed to reintegrate a feminine perspective into Christian theology.

Nevertheless, I've often thought that if there's one single myth which encapsulates the fundamental distinction between Eastern and Western religion, it's the story of Adam and Eve. In Judaism, Christianity and Islam, the quest for divine knowledge must be prevented at all costs. "If they eat of the tree," God complains in Genesis, "they will become godlike, like us." Throughout the millennia, mystics who appeared in these cultures were often persecuted. In Eastern religions such as Hinduism and Buddhism however, as well as in classical Western civilization, this quest was the whole point of life, and was to be pursued at all costs. Mystics in these cultures were honored and even deified, and methods for attaining states of consciousness allowing one to penetrate the veil of duality—the numerous techniques of yoga—were perfected and widely taught. What a contrast! To this very day the Roman Catholic pope still actively condemns even so basic a spiritual exercise as meditation.

For the Westerner, eating that apple is the worst possible sin; questioning why God would deny us a share in his divine nature is the worst possible blasphemy. For the Easterner, not reaching for that apple is the greatest spiritual failure. The tree, of course, is the spinal column, and the serpent wound around it is the force of *kundalini,* the Goddess' own presence in our bodies, which gives both knowledge and life. The image of two snakes (*ida* and *pingala,* the right and left currents of *kundalini shakti)* wrapped around a wand, representing the rising of spiritual awareness, was common to the Hindu, Chaldean, Greek and Roman civilizations. But we in the West were forbidden to eat of the tree of inner awareness, and the true significance of this sacred image was lost for us. Of these four great ancient civilizations, working knowledge of the inner forces of enlightenment has survived on a mass scale only in India. Only in India has the inner tradition of the Goddess endured. This is the reason the teachings of India are so precious. They offer us a glimpse of what our own ancient wisdom must have been. The Indians have preserved our lost heritage.

GRANDMOTHER OF THE WORLD

"East is East and West is West," wrote Rudyard Kipling, but what exactly is "East"? Kipling joined most Europeans in grouping India with the East, but perhaps this is a flawed distinction. Much of what we call the West today consists of a wide assortment of ethnic groups speaking primarily Indo-European languages (English, German, French, Italian, etc.) and practicing Near Eastern-based religions (Christianity, Islam and Judaism). Greater India is the one culture which speaks Indo-European languages (Hindi, Bengali, Gujarati, Nepalese, etc.) and still practices an Indo-European religion (Hinduism).

According to the *Rig Veda,* in extremely remote times large numbers of Hindus migrated northwest out of the subcontinent, spreading Sanskrit-related languages throughout Central Asia, the Middle East, and Europe. The *Rig Veda,* composed at least 6000 years ago, names migrant waves who left India: the Parshus (Persians), Prithus (Parthians), Bhrigus (perhaps the Phrygians), and Alinas, who some scholars speculate were the ancestors of the Hellenes, that is, the Greeks. Some even wonder whether the Druhyus, described as leaving India in very early times, may have been the ancestors of the Druids. All these groups had languages and religions closely related to those of India. India may well be the grandmother of the world. The prototype of many of our Western goddesses may well still live in Indian temples, honored by the Hindus now as they were by our own Western ancestors in remote antiquity.

THE CALL OF ISIS

In India, Goddess worship has always coexisted comfortably with God worship. In some sects, such as the Vaishnava, God is primary; his wife serves him lovingly and devotedly. In other sects, such as the Shaktas, the Goddess is primary, and may or may not take a male consort. In still others, the absolute equivalence of the two genders is strongly emphasized, such as the Shaiva sects which make a point to represent God/dess as half male, half female (Ardha Shiva).

In Egypt also, Isis and Osiris were worshiped both together and separately. The ancient Egyptians had a great deal in common with the Hindus: a caste-based society, a powerful sacerdotal class, reverence for the cow as a symbol of gentle nurturance, and even an annual festival of lights celebrating the Goddess just as Hindus do on Divali, their most important holiday. In the first century A.D., Apollonius, a physician from Tyana, after visiting both India and Egypt, concluded that a group of Indians must have migrated to North Africa long, long ago, and that the Egyptian priests and desert ascetics preserved part of this Hindu legacy. How else to explain the remarkable similarities between the yogis of India and the famous Egyptian gymnosophists?

The Egyptian faith centering around the worship of Isis spread far beyond the borders of North Africa throughout the Mediterranean and northeast into Europe. Lucius Apuleius's second century novel, *Metamorphoses* (Transformations), transports us into the world of Isis. His funny but disastrously unlucky hero is a glutton and rake who has heard much about the spiritual powers of women, but experiences them first hand when a prostitute transforms him into a donkey. The second half of the novel describes his misadventures in the body of an ass—even his old horse mistreats him! Apuleius humorously makes the point that unbridled pursuit of sensual pleasure makes asses of all of us.

The last few chapters of the *Metamorphoses* change dramatically in tone, however, as our luckless hero begins to understand how he brought this disaster on himself and sincerely repents. Many scholars agree that these pages, describing the animal-man's plea to the Goddess for grace and forgiveness, constitute one of the most unique and valuable documents to have survived from this era, especially since it describes initiation into Isis' mysteries in some detail. It begins:

> Weeping with sorrow and despair, I cried out to the all powerful Goddess: Queen of heaven, whether you are Mother Ceres who generously feeds all your creatures here on earth, whether you are Venus who brings men and women together in order to populate the world, whether you are Diana who lights up the night and brings to women in labor a speedy recovery, whether you are Proserpine who through your bitter wailings frighten away the evil spirits who assail us, by whatever name or form or system of belief men and women call on you, I too call to you for mercy! Please forgive me and forgive also my enemies, for having suffered so much myself, I cannot bear to see anyone else suffer either. Please save me from my animal body and allow me to resume my true form.

The ass finally falls asleep and has the most astonishing dream. Rising out of the sea emerges a lustrous female form, crowned with flowers, wearing a dress the color of variegated blossoms, and covered with a black cloak on which the moon and stars shine. In her right hand she holds a musical instrument which continuously sounds three glorious notes.

"My son," the woman speaks, "I have come. Know that I am the mother of all things, empress of the divine powers, and queen of the elements. I am one being only, yet I am worshiped in the forms of numberless gods and goddesses. The Phrygians call me the Mother of the Gods, the Athenians call me Minerva, the Cyprians call me Venus, the Cretians, Diana, the Sicilians, Proserpine, the Eleusians, Ceres. I am called Juno and Hecate and many other names here and in the Orient. The Egyptians, masters of the ancient doctrine, hail me as Queen Isis."

Isis consoles the animal-man and advises him to watch for a certain priest at the following day's Goddess festival. He is then to trot up behind him and eat the roses the priest is carrying. Isis reassures him that she will always be with him, for her grace is always free to those who call out to her with love and sincerity, even from the bottommost depths of hell. Our hero follows her instructions and the priest—who has been alerted in a vision to watch for a hungry donkey!—restores his humanity.

Thus our glutton and rake escapes the fate his animal-like behavior called down on himself. "Fate has no power against those who serve and honor the Goddess," he concludes. "They are safe from every foe and misfortune who honor the one Goddess whose radiance gives light to the gods themselves." Our hero, thoroughly transformed, is initiated by the priest in a beautiful, elaborate ritual, and spends the rest of his life continuing to purify himself and serving the divine force.

How can we in the West resurrect our lost heritage and reconnect with the living Goddess so that we, like our ancient ancestors, can also purify ourselves and serve her? The first obstacle we have to face is that we don't really believe in her. For many of us she remains a myth, a concept, or merely a feminist icon. She may live for the village people of India, but she doesn't live for us. We don't really see her in the world or in our lives, much less within ourselves. "You can't see electricity," says Ammachi, a contemporary saint of southwest India, "but if you touch a live wire, you will definitely feel it. You may not be able to see the Divine Mother, but if you still your mind and open your heart, you will definitely feel her!"

We may sit shivering in front of a pile of wood, wishing all night long it would catch fire and warm us, but if someone ignites our kindling with a burning fagot brought from their campfire, our stack of wood will start to burn instantly. In India the divine light of the Mother of the Universe still blazes as brightly as it did ten thousand years ago. The Hindus have a vast, ancient, and unspeakably profound tradition of the Divine Mother, and they are happy to share the warm fire of their wisdom with us (though, unlike the missionaries of the West, they never force their tradition on others).

The Goddess wisdom of India is, after all, not just a Hindu tradition; it was the tradition of the entire world not so very long ago. The Shaktas of India can remind us how we used to perform the Goddess's rites ourselves not so many centuries in the past, and re-awaken our memories of the deeper understanding we used to have of who and what the Divine Mother really is. They can reintroduce us to the disciplines necessary to honor the Mother and to prepare ourselves, our society and our planet for her triumphal return. In a moment's time their profound insights can scoop us beyond our own limited vision of the Goddess, restoring her original unlimited glory not only as an Earth Mother but as the One in the palm of whose hand trillions of universes rest like grains of dust. They can carry us beyond psychological interpretations, theological formulations and archeological recreations into the limitless divine awareness of the eternal, blissful, ever living Goddess.

At the end of the 19th century, extraordinary men from India such as Swami Vivekananda came to the West to introduce us to yoga, the science of divine realization. At the end of the 20th century, extraordinary women from India such as Ammachi, Shree Maa of Kamakhya, Meera Ma and Karunamayi Ma, began coming to the West to introduce us to the inner essence of yoga practice: the living Goddess herself. The men brought us to the portal, the women introduce us to the Goddess within. There is no doubt in my mind that these Hindu women will have an impact on Western spirituality in the 21st century as great or greater than that the Hindu men had in the 20th century. The men primed us for the revelation; the women are bringing the living presence of the Goddess to restore a balanced spirituality to the West, a spirituality that embraces the feminine as well as the masculine, and that looks beyond the religious belief inculcated in the West to the spiritual experience cultivated in the East.

Two thousand years of male dominated religion is enough. The 21st century is dawning. It's time to tear down the No Trespassing sign from the Garden of Eden, find those forbidden trees and fearlessly eat the fruit of Knowledge and Life. Mother Sophia is waiting.

In the past 2,000 years, Christians and Muslims, and most recently the Communists, conspired to wipe our memories clean of tens of thousands of years of Goddess spirituality in the Americas, Africa, Europe, the Middle East, Central and East Asia, and Australia. I offer this book as a small token of my overwhelming gratitude to the people of India, who in spite of continual invasions by hostile cultures seeking to impose their own religions on the subcontinent, fought to keep the light of the inner traditions of the Mother of the Universe alive. I bow especially to the masters, the great yogis and yoginis, who embodied the Mother's light in their own lives, and demonstrated by their own example the possibility of the enlightened life. Again and again I offer my loving respect to the Shakta teachers who took me and my husband under their care and brought us into the living presence of the Mother Divine.

I would like to conclude by quoting from one of the most poignant Goddess texts I've ever read. *Thunder, Perfect Mind,* a portion of which is summarized here, was preserved among the manuscripts found at Nag Hammadi in Egypt. It represents the words of Isis at the beginning of the Christian era, just as the West began to turn away from the Mother of the Universe, replacing a world in which God and Goddess had equal share with a new order in which only a male deity was sanctioned. "Don't forget me!" Isis cries. "Remember me always!" The Mother of the Universe is speaking. It behooves us to listen.

We Westerners have inherited a drastically impoverished world-view in which the Goddess, and all the cherished feminine values and rich inner experience her worship entails, have been lost. According to the ancient Egyptians, when her husband Osiris was lost, Isis set out to find the scattered parts of his body and restore him. Today it up to us to locate and restore the tradition of the living Goddess. We would do well to begin our search in India, where for not one moment in all of human history have the children of the living Goddess forgotten their Divine Mother.

THUNDER, PERFECT MIND

The Goddess to the Children of the West:

I come from infinite Power
    to those who meditate on me.
I am found by those who seek sincerely.
Gaze on me in your meditation;
    still your thoughts, and listen to me.
Those of you who wait for me,
    stop waiting! Receive me now!
Don't ever turn away from me.
Don't forget me in any moment, in any place.
Stay alert! Remember me always!

I am the first and the last,
    the one who is honored and the one who is spit upon,
    the priestess and the whore.

I am the wife and the virgin,
 the barren woman with numberless sons.
I am the bride and also the groom,
 the mother of my father,
  my husband's sister—and his daughter.
I am the incomprehensible silence.
The sound of my silence has produced the universe.
I am the sound of my name.

Don't laugh at me when I am thrown out,
 don't mock my fall.
Don't forsake me, though I am weak,
 and do not fear my all encompassing power.
I am the one who exists in your fear,
 the strength in your quaking limbs.

Why do you hate me, children of the West?
Because I am from a foreign culture?
I am the wisdom of the Egyptians,
 and your wisdom too.
My image is worshiped in Egypt
 though I exist beyond all images.
Throughout the world, people hate me,
 and everywhere my blessings are gratefully accepted.

I am the force the Egyptians call Life,
 but whom you call Death.
I am the one the Egyptians call Law
 but whom you have rejected as a criminal.
I am the one before whom you were once ashamed to stand,
 and now you treat me contemptuously.
I am the one you call ignorance,
 though I taught you everything.
You have turned away from me
 but wherever you go, I stand before you.

I am the one who seeks
and I am the knowledge I seek.

I am the inner strength of the angels and gods,
    and of the men and women who dwell in me.
I am perfect peace
    but war erupts because of me.
I am the shape of all things
    though I have no shape.
Those who reject me, dwell in ignorance.
Those who have made themselves one with my essence,
    know me entirely.
Yet those who are closest to me don't know me at all
    and those who are furthest from me live in me always.
Come to me like little children.

I control the universe
    but I am uncontrollable.
I am the changeless, and I am always changing.
I am the one beneath you
    but you must ascend to me.
I am absolute purity
    yet evil arises out of me.
My outer expression is raging lust,
    my inner expression is perfect self control.
I am the sounds everyone hears
    but no one understands what I say.

The reality inside you is the reality with which you
    surround yourself,
    and what you see around yourself
    is what you created within you.
You plot against me,
    yet I alone exist
    and there is no one to judge me.
How delightful sin is, the lies, the passion,
    the intensity of pleasure.
But when you tire of yourself, come sit quietly,
    for I am there inside you.
And when you find me you will live,
    and never die again.

A Shakta Catechism

Consciousness is.
She is blissful and self-aware.
She knows, wills, and acts.
She creates, maintains, and destroys.
She deludes and enlightens.

With an infinitesimal fraction of her power,
she emanates the universes.
Time, space, and causation emerge from her.
She herself is unbounded.
Matter emerges from her. Matter is not material.

All of this is her energy.
All of this is the movement of her will.
She is universal intelligence,
the invisible organizing field governing all visible things.

Her word is the primal vibration.
Mantras are the echoes of her song.

The universe is her yantra.
The body is her yantra.
This yantra is that yantra.

She incarnates as the cosmos.
She incarnates as life.
She incarnates as the guru.
She incarnates in the images in which she is invoked.
Women are the incarnations of the Goddess.
Men are also her incarnations.

She intervenes in history.
She nurtures and illumines.
She disciplines and terrifies.
She guides and blesses.
All living things are her children.
Everything is sacred.

All this is her play.
All this is her delight.
All this is her grace.

About the Author

At fourteen, Linda Johnsen was caught in a soulquake. Everything she thought she knew about life, religion, and reality itself cracked apart as the Mother of the Universe stepped into her life. This completely unexpected and (unfortunately) unrepeated mystical experience propelled her on a frantic search, leading Linda to the yogis and yoginis, pandits and saints of India, by whom she was initiated in the Shaktadvaita tradition of the Great Goddess.

Today Linda spends much of her time shuttling back and forth between Eastern and Western realities. She is particularly interested in the Hellenistic period, when Western civilization shared many of the insights and practices preserved in the East until this day. She earned a Master's degree in Eastern Studies, has done post-graduate work in Comparative Religions, and has been especially active in introducing Jyotish, one of India's most advanced yogic systems, to a Western audience.

Linda has published over one hundred articles on Eastern spirituality. Her essays have appeared in a half dozen anthologies including *The Divine Mosaic: Women's Images of the Sacred Other* and *Uncoiling the Snake: Ancient Patterns in Contemporary Women's Lives.* Her previous book, *Daughters of the Goddess: The Women Saints of India,* received the Midwest Book Association award for "Best New Age Book of the Year."

Linda lives in Kali-fornia (California) with husband Johnathan Brown, student of Eastern and Western sciences.

Other Books from Yes International Publishers

YOGA AND SPIRITUALITY:

Daughters of the Goddess: The Women Saints of India
    Linda Johnsen

Walking with a Himalayan Master: An American;s Odyssey
    Justin O'Brien

A Meeting of Mystic Paths: Christianity and Yoga
    Justin O'Brien

The Yogi: Portraits of Swami Vishnu-devananda
    Gopala Krishna

SELF-TRANSFORMATION:

Pigs Eat Wolves: Going into Partnership with Your Dark Side
    Charles Bates

The Wellness Tree: Six Step Program for Optimal Health
    Justin O'Brien

Ransoming the Mind: Yoga and Modern Therapy
    Charles Bates

WOMEN'S SPIRITUALITY:

The Spiral Path: Explorations in Women's Spirituality
    Theresa King

The Divine Mosaic: Women's Images of the Sacred Other
    Theresa King

Circle of Mysteries: The Women's Rosary Book
    Christin Lore Weber

INSPIRATIONAL POETRY:

The Light of Ten Thousand Suns
    Swami Veda Bharati

Soulfire: Love Poems in Black and Gold
    Alla Renee Bozarth

Call or write for a book catalog or copy of Yes News & Views:
Yes International Publishers
1317 Summit Avenue • St. Paul, MN 55105-2602
651-645-6808